ANGELS ON MY PATH

Kagabo **Ka**yiranga (Kaka) Jean-Léonard

with Max T. Russell

Dear Kim,

Thank you for reading my story.
Feel free to share with friends and
family.

Jean Leonard Kagabo Kaka.

Direct inquiries to:

Max and Max Communications
Box 141
New Palestine, IN 46163

Or write the authors at: KagaboRussell@gmail.com

Published in the United States of America by Max and Max Communications, New Palestine, Indiana

ISBN: 9781792910883

DEDICATIONS

Kaka's:

To my mother, my father, my brothers and sisters

To the massacred Tutsis who cannot tell their own stories

To the brave Hutus who were harmed or murdered for helping Tutsis, their fellow Rwandans

To the RPF soldiers who gave or risked their lives to stop the bloodshed

To the survivors who are still physically and mentally affected by the violence, betrayal and loss

To readers who are affected by violence

Max's:

To Zaiyn Jacob and your siblings to follow

CONTENTS

ACKNOWLEDGMENTS

Thanks to Max for his assistance in composing and writing my story, and to my siblings who helped me reassemble our history in ways my memory alone would have not been able to do. It can be unpleasant, but we all know how important it is to remember what happened and how we moved forward together, even though our path to recovery from the atrocities and our losses was not clear. Despite our disappointments, we have plenty to laugh about and plenty of good memories to pass on to our children. I thank Kaliza and other survivors who have shared details that support the book. Thanks to my wife Diane for allowing me to take time out of our busy daily schedule in order to complete this task. I thank God for giving me the strength, the courage and the resources to be able to write this book.
—Kaka

Thanks to the Kagabos for letting me snoop around in your minds to find what was in there, even when you said it wasn't there. And thanks for letting me cross-examine what we found. Thanks to my good amigo Robert Rand Eberwein for your excellent literary guidance and for being a testing ground for weak stomachs. And thanks to Rosikjan Russell Boze, whose expertise in the history of the Armenian genocide made me understand the method and the loss of genocide, and prepared me to pull Kaka's story out of him, bit by bit.

—Max

CO-AUTHOR'S NOTE

I met Kaka on a country road that cuts through fields of corn and soybeans. His car was out of gas in the same spot where my Mitsubishi van died once upon a time. His indigenous features told me he was from an African nation I wasn't very familiar with. On the way to a gas station, I asked which one. He said, "Rwanda," and I said, "Oh." He bought a gas can at the station and filled it up, and as we walked to my car I blurted, "Rwanda! We have to talk about forgiveness and reconciliation!" He said, "I think we need another word for reconciliation."

That's when I knew I was talking to a realistic man. It's easy for Americans to applaud all the post-genocide forgiving and reconciling going on over in Rwanda, but it is in fact limited and tough going. Extremists have invented propaganda to fool people into believing that the 1994 genocide that knocked off 1,074,017 Tutsis in Rwanda[1] never actually happened, or that it was followed by a vengeful genocide against Hutus.

Kaka didn't want his part of that history to be forgotten. He told me shortly after we met that he wanted his children to know his story. But he didn't have any children, not even a wife. I told him I'd help him write the story, not realizing it would turn into a big project. We spent many months excavating his and some of his siblings' memories and making sense of them. There are ways to access accurate memories, and honesty has little to do with it. Much of my life has been spent observing this from a background in human learning and memory, digging seemingly nonexistent information out of people's heads, often without their knowing it.

Kaka's head turned out to be full of story, a very interesting series of episodes marked by unpleasant interruptions. It's what he and I discovered together, along with his family's memories. Any errors of fact and any names that might be confused with people outside his story are unintentional. I expect more memories and information to trickle in for years to come, perfecting this book. We changed the names of a few victims and perpetrators.

As far as I can tell, this is the first autobiography to focus on a Tutsi boy survivor's childhood and his experience in the entire genocide – in Rwanda, not as a refugee or portrayed along with adult memoirs. Several other Tutsi males have written powerful memoirs, but these either technically are not autobiographies or do not dwell on childhood.

By the way, Kaka and I make Hutu and Tutsi plural by adding an *s*. That might bother some people.

—Max T. Russell

[1]This number was obtained from *Ministry of Local Government, Good Governance, Community Development and Social Affairs* (MINALOC), Kigali, April 2004. The estimate echoed in most publications is 800,000, an amazing sum, to be sure, but Rwandan officials and survivors had the time and motivation to perform a stricter count.

KAKA'S NOTE

This isn't a religious book. I just believe God preserved me to tell a certain story that others cannot tell, either because they were killed or because something inside them was killed. I actually believe real angels from heaven watched over me for this purpose.

Some reconciliation is happening in Rwanda. It's a long, difficult process. More relatives of the perpetrators are attending commemoration events and visiting genocide memorial sites. Some are helping survivors in different ways. In addition, Rwanda police report fewer cases of genocide denial and ideology. So, there's been some progress.

Twenty-five years is not a long time for healing. It takes a great deal of courage for killers (and the many people who assisted them or cheered them on) to admit their guilt. It must be terribly painful to face the truth about themselves, and then to say it out loud. I look forward to the day when the perpetrators or their families acknowledge the hideous crimes and ask if I can find it in my heart to forgive them. It will be good for us all.

— Kagabo Kayiranga Jean-Léonard

WHAT PAPA SAID

My father was a farmer and a school principal. My mother was a sixth-grade teacher. I was the tenth of twelve children. We were Tutsis and, as far I knew, we lived in peace with our Hutu neighbors, many of whom had farms too. We all spoke Kinyarwanda, the national language of Rwanda.

My family wasn't wealthy, but we had five cows, three goats, ten chickens, and more than a hundred acres of land in various locations. There was always work to be done. Even though my family was large enough to handle our own needs, my parents kept a hired hand around to help with chores on school days. We kept our cows in a shed at night, and in the morning the helper let them out to graze in a nearby field of eucalyptus trees. If the grass in that field needed to grow back, he walked them several miles to one of our other pastures.

Fetching water at what we called *the fountain* was a central part of life. The fountain supplied most of the neighborhood's water for drinking, cooking, cleaning and bathing. We had to go after the water ourselves when the hired hand was sick and when we were on summer vacation. We used yellow, plastic containers with caps screwed on them that held several gallons. To get to the fountain, you had to go around our fence to a path that led between our neighbors' houses, take a left on the path and continue until you came to where it went down and then curved to the right. You kept going until it curved to the left, descending the whole time, and then you turned left again and kept walking for a while before you turned right and ended up on the main road of our town, Kimisange. The road was paved with dirt, and you followed it to a moderately steep path down to the watering hole, the fountain that never ran dry.

It was a horizontal, six-inch-wide plastic pipe that barely poked out of the elevated ground behind it. Twenty feet farther back was a circular, concrete tank. Except for its metal cover, it was entirely underground. All children were instructed never to remove the cover or dirt might fall in. We weren't even supposed to get near it, but I raised the lid now and then and saw that the tank was full of clear water. Water ran continuously out of the pipe, which was just high enough that we could stand our tall containers under it. We all took turns fetching water this way. Most people carried one container – sometimes a bucket – home on their head, steadying it with a hand. If they were strong enough, they carried another container with their free hand. You had to be careful how much water you balanced or you'd hurt your neck and back. To protect your head, you shaped banana leaves into a green, donut-like cushion and set the container on it. That cushion made all the difference in the world during the walk home.

The soil around the fountain was sandy and full of cold water. I could see earthworms in it, and when I stepped in I couldn't actually feel the worms, and they didn't bite, but I knew I was stepping on them. Watching the soil ooze through my toes was gross.

Water flowed out of the pipe and down a ten-foot-long cement channel and onto the ground, forming a shallow pool around the fountain system. Our cows liked the fountain and they didn't mind the worms. We took our water from the pipe, they took theirs from the runoff. Some of them didn't mind blocking our way to the pipe or jabbing us with their long horns. We learned to let them finish drinking at their own pace and get out of our way so we could fill our containers.

One of our cows distinguished herself with exceptionally good manners that earned her the name, Inka Y'ineza. It means "Nice (and Well Behaved) Cow." I loved Nice Cow. I loved watching her graze. I loved petting her as she chewed the grass. I loved watching Uncle Nicodem milk her, and I loved watching her calves nurse on her. Inka Y'ineza was brown, the oldest of our little herd, and she produced the most calves. I was always interested in watching our cows give birth. We kept the calves in a shed to protect them from the blistering sun. I looked forward to sunset, when we would let them run around our house and our entire yard, bursting with energy, playing and kicking up their legs.

I'll tell you something that proves how much I loved Nice Cow. My Aunt Josephine said that when she visited our home, she would call me to sit and talk with her, and I would say, "No way! I'd rather hang out with Inka Y'ineza and Uncle Nicodem."

We butchered Nice Cow after she quit giving milk. We kept some of the meat and sold the rest to our neighbors. She died a natural death, as I recall, but not all our cows did. An elderly, local, uneducated neighbor diagnosed them when they were sick or they died too soon. He once performed an autopsy while we were butchering a cow that had died prematurely. He examined the intestines and said the cause of death was steel-hard intestines – impacted feces. He had an explanation for everything, and we always wondered how he knew what he claimed to know.

Our hired hand helped with cooking too. We employed only one hired man at a time and we enjoyed the company of the different men who filled that position. Some stayed on for up to five years. They lived with us during the school year because they came from so far away. These were Hutus we already knew or who were referred by people we knew.

The men did not babysit us. Women were hired for that, and my mom was glad to have them for house cleaning. They did most of the laundry too. My older sisters occasionally washed a small load at home, but that did not prevent the dirty clothes from accumulating to frightening proportions every three weeks. The amount of water needed for large loads demanded a trip to the fountain. Either my sisters or the helpers would wrap the laundry in a large bed sheet, tie the four corners together, and set out for the fountain. It took thirty minutes to haul it there. It took the same amount of time to carry water or the clean laundry back to the house.

Washing our clothes at the fountain took several hours and two plastic tubs – one green, one red. They were round, twenty-four inches across, eight inches deep. First, you filled the tubs with water and soaked a few articles of clothing in one of them. You rubbed a bar of soap into the fabric and then worked the fabric against the lower part of your thumb, adding a powder stain remover as needed. Next, you put those clothes in the other tub, rinsed them once or twice, wrung them out and then shook out the wrinkles. Finally, the clothes were spread out on a section of grass to dry. The fountain was a popular place, so you had to keep an eye on your clothes, in order not to mix them up with other people's articles or lose them to thieves.

I didn't have as many clothes as my brothers did, since I didn't have underwear until I was in second grade. I realized the injustice one day at age five when I saw my older brothers stripped down to their bare necessities. I asked my mom to buy me some undies. She reduced the problem to four simple words: "You don't need them."

We never lost any clothing at the fountain, but I did have to defend myself against a certain bully who enjoyed picking on people. My older brothers asked me why the boy was so pushy. They said they thought I could beat him up. So, when he came by to pick on me – or perhaps my brothers invited him – I beat him up, which involved rolling on the ground until I was on top and he couldn't get up. I was seven and I wasn't going to let another seven-year-old get the best of me if my brothers said he couldn't.

After the clothes had dried, they were folded and carried home in the same bed sheet. Chores never ended, and the hired help made it possible for my mother to be in the classroom and for us kids to spend more time on homework. My mom liked teaching. She had been at it since graduating from high school at age eighteen. The hired help respected her and my father and were grateful for a job. Our helpers came from countryside settlements where employment was mighty scarce. Even my town had neither plumbing nor electricity, but my family and many of our neighbors were rich compared to the helpers we hired.

My mother was queen of home and farm. She made sure the cooks were cooking the right food for us kids, and she made sure we did our chores. When she had time to work in the fields with the farmhands, and with us at harvest or during vacations, she supervised while she worked. Above all, she and Papa encouraged us to study hard. I could not see the future they saw when Papa periodically reminded us, "Everything you are doing you are doing for your own sakes, not for mine, because one of these days I will not be around, and you will be taking care of yourselves."

MEET MY FAMILY

Big families have lots of names to keep straight, and ours were kind of complicated. Since last names go first in our native language, my father was Kagabo Jean-Nepomuscene and my mother was Mukankuranga Adele. When I was growing up, I thought all my brothers and sisters were her biological children, because we all called her Maman Paul, as our father instructed us to do. Maman is French for mom, and my parents really liked French.

Most of my brothers and sisters lived at home until they finished sixth grade. Then they either went away to boarding school or they attended a high school near home. There were never more than ten children living at home, including cousins. When the *abicanyi* (ah-BEE-chah-NYEE) burned down my maternal grandmother's house in 1992, we opened ours to her and five of my cousins. But I'm getting ahead of myself. I need to explain the earlier years.

Before I was born, my father lived with his first wife in a village called Mutoyi, in the greater Kigali district. Kigali is the capital of Rwanda, pronounced as "Rhonda" in Kinyarwanda. My father's wife died shortly after giving birth to their sixth child, a boy named Ingabire. Papa was awfully lonely after his wife's death. Going to work every day to support his family while everyone was grieving must have been difficult beyond imagination. Then he met my mother and was happy again. They married several months later, she moved in with him, and that's how Maman Paul became the only mother Ingabire ever knew.

If you're doing the math, you've figured out that Papa had six children by his first wife and another six by the second. He had a custom for naming Kagabo kids. About a week after one was born, and while the family was gathered around the dinner table, he invited suggestions for a name. It must've been a game because, after all suggestions were made, he would announce the legal name and a nickname, and they were never anything we recommended. The first six children, from oldest to youngest, are as follows.

Gasanabo. Full name: Gasanabo Jean-Damascene. We called him by his "last" name, a combination of letters and syllables from his mother's last name, Musanabera, and Papa's last name, Kagabo. Nickname: Volks, when he was a small child. It was short for Volkswagen. His nickname changed to Damas (duh-MAHS) over time.

Damas moved to Switzerland to pursue an advanced degree in education when I was four or five, and he stayed there for more than twenty years. After the 1994 killings, he and Jean-Marie and Polie (whom I will introduce momentarily) sent money from overseas to help care for those of us who survived. It was great to see Damas on his occasional visits home, because I didn't remember anything about him before that. He was just a picture in the family album that was destroyed when Hutu extremists destroyed our home.

Since the abicanyi didn't get Damas, I have many new memories and pictures of him. He earned a Ph.D. in education and returned to our homeland to work for the government.

Standard. (stan-DAH, with a slight gutteral scrape). Full name: Kagabo Jean-Bosco. Nickname: Standard. I had much more knowledge of him than I had of Gasanabo when I was a kid. Standard became a veterinarian when I was seven, and rented an apartment about twenty minutes from home. During his frequent visits to our house, he helped Papa educate and discipline the rest of us. He encouraged us to read and love the French language. He had us read French-language magazines and newspapers out loud to him. He kept track of our report cards. He scolded us when we slacked off in our studies, and he rewarded us with whatever we wanted when our grades were good. He gave me my first soccer ball! We normally made a ball out of layers of plastic bags wrapped into a big, tight glob, but this one was official. My other brothers thought I was crazy to choose a soccer ball over a pair of expensive shoes, but I loved soccer, and my brothers were glad about my choice every time they borrowed it.

Standard bought me a pair of jeans and my all-time favorite shirt for looking after two goats that he kept at our farm. He took me for rides on his Yamaha motorcycle. We walked to the stadium together to watch professional soccer matches that were as grand as the Super Bowl. He was like a father to me. The abicanyi went to his apartment and stole his mattress and radio and told him they'd come back in a few days to get him.

Pigeon (pee-ZHONE, with a French nasal ending that gets lost in your nose, so that the *n* is not actually pronounced). Full name: Kagabo Jean-Marie. Nickname: Pigeon. Jean-Marie is a typical French name. I don't know how his nickname became Pigeon. I only know that nobody called him by his birth name. But now that I think of it, nobody called any of us, except Gasanabo and Ingabire, by our first names.

Pigeon liked to keep us younger kids occupied with songs and games while the cooks prepared dinner. It usually wasn't ready until nine o'clock in the evening, and by then we younger ones were worn out and ready to fall asleep after all the day's activities. He made sure we stayed awake long enough to eat dinner, because it would have been too difficult to wake us up again, even if we knew dinner was waiting. Pigeon was twenty-eight and had just finished his B.A. in political philosophy in the Congo when the abicanyi came.

Polie (poh-LEE). Full name: Kagabo Ilibagiza Marie Rose. Nickname: Polie, French for *polite*. She is one of the twins. By my parents' estimation, she was an exceptionally well-behaved daughter. By a younger brother's measure, she was not as impressive as Nice Cow. Polie was annoyed by the soccer games my brothers and I played outside when the ball bounced against the window of the room where she studied. One day, after the ball hit the window, she put her books down long enough to come outside and order us to stop our game. We ignored her and continued playing.

The ball hit the window again. Polie came out and slapped my brother, Leaticau. He was ten; she was a high school junior. He responded with disrespectful opinions that made Polie cry, and for that he received a spanking when my father came home from work. So, you see, he got a slap, a spanking and a quick lesson about underestimating the value of learning and about bad-mouthing his sister. Nice Cow never caused that kind of commotion.

Polie was studying law in Switzerland when the genocide started. She later moved to the state of Indiana, USA, and sponsored me to come over on a student visa. True to form, she sternly warned me that I would have to study and work hard to make it here.

Jolie (zhoh-LEE) Full name: Kagabo Ihogoza Marie Louise. Nickname: Jolie, French for *cute*. She and Polie were twins, equal in beauty.

Jolie attended a boarding school five hours from home. Whenever she came back on break, she spoiled us younger siblings with candy, cookies and bubble gum and spent time with us. She didn't boss us around like Polie did.

The twins were close friends and helped each other with chores. Jolie graduated after fourteenth grade – the senior year of what was called high school but was partly college – and then moved back home and taught fifth grade at Kivugiza, where Papa was principal for a year before transferring to a school near home where Maman Paul taught. At long last, Jolie had spending money and she used part of it to buy me a pair of shoes to replace the ones I had worn out around home.

Ingabire (eengah-BEE-reh; trill the *r* once), African for *gift from God*. That is, in the weighty grief of losing a wife, my father gained a son. Full name: Kagabo Ingabire Jean-Paul. Nickname: none given, perhaps due to the disruption his birth caused when his birth mother died. By custom, mothers are usually called by their first child's name. When Papa remarried, my mother adopted part of Ingabire's name because he was still a baby and, in a sense, the first of her children. Thus she became Maman Paul.

Ingabire was one of the taller family members and was the oldest brother at home during my childhood. He was responsible for taking care of our cows after school with the help of us younger brothers. We accompanied him to fetch grass for the cattle to eat and sleep on. The grass was thick and tall, and the cows liked it fresh. We cut it with machetes. One of us would chop enough to feed the cows for one evening, while another tied the stalks into bundles. We carried the bundles on our heads back to the stable where the cows would eat for an hour and then lie down to sleep.

As our supervisor, Ingabire also made sure we stayed busy during vacation by tending to the cows and goats. We took them out to graze, we cleaned and dried the grass they slept on – which became wet and soggy from the cows' waste – and sometimes we had to go and find grass from the field for fresh bedding. Ingabire saw to it that we three younger brothers did our part of the tedious and tiring chores. One day I refused to help after school. I said, "Why don't you do it yourself?" He did the work without me, and that evening I received a memorable punishment from Papa for disobeying my older brother.

Ingabire was not the kind of person to stand around and do nothing when there was work to be done…or when help was needed to rescue Tutsis from Hutu extremists who wanted to erase every last one of us from the face of the earth.

Now I'll introduce the six children born to my mother, Maman Paul, whom we often addressed as Ma Paul (ma-POH).

Leaticau (LEH-tee-koh). Full name: Kagabo Nkuranga Jean-Pierre. Nickname: Leaticau, taken from Laetitia, Latin for joy or happiness. My older siblings said he got sick a lot during his toddler years. Leaticau was always an example of scholarship. I was expected to rank only in the top ten of my class, whereas my parents expected Leuticau to always be first in his. Although he had little room for improvement, I think he was rewarded nevertheless, because I noticed he often went on visits far and near to relatives and friends of the family. His hard work and performance earned him my parents' permission to attend soccer's World Cup. I admired him for that and was inspired to study hard.

Leaticau shared his monthly college scholarship allowance with me during my high school years, after the killings. I could go to him when I needed food, clothes and other provisions. He reached out to older siblings for additional support and they sent it to him to distribute to survivors in the family as he saw fit. Leaticau and I spent a lot of time together during the genocide.

Kigingi (tchee-JEEN-jee). Full name: Kagabo Rangira Jean-Baptiste. Nickname: Rwandans call him Rangira (lahn-JEE-ruh, with the second *r* trilled). He goes by JB (Jean-Baptiste) here in America. I will call him Rangira in this story, and when I do, try to hear the correct pronunciation in your mind.

Rangira was four years older than I. All of us in the family were good at soccer, but he was the best, probably because he played so much. By fourth grade, he was sneaking away from our yard at every chance to play soccer or ride a bike. Sometimes people would tell my parents they had seen him riding far into other neighborhoods on a bike which my parents knew was not his since they had not bought him one, and Papa would give him several whacks with a switch made from a small branch. That encouraged my brother to sneak away more carefully. The time would come when Papa would make stronger attempts to keep us kids from spending much time at the homes of people who would become our assasins.

Much as Rangira loved soccer, he loved riding a bicycle even more. In fact, he was the only child in the family who knew how. Bikes were expensive, and summer vacation brought the temptation to ride. Rangira often managed to save enough money to rent a bike from the few kids in our neighborhood who owned one. Depending on how much money Rangira had, he would rent the bike for an hour or a certain number of minutes. It was quite a sight to see someone on a bike, so Rangira was sure to be noticed as he pedaled through the streets.

He was seventeen during the genocide and was the last of the family to see…well, I'll get to that later.

Dada (dah-DAH). Full name: Kagabo Umugwaneza Marie-Claire. Nickname: Dada, which means *sister* in Kinyarwanda. She was quiet, perhaps the kindest of us kids. She was a good student, as good as Leaticau, and she always obeyed my parents. My siblings and I teased her for not liking beef or chicken, but we didn't complain. It left more for us at mealtime. Dada never got in trouble for kicking a soccer ball into a window or sneaking off our property or smarting off to older siblings. She didn't get in trouble for anything, because she never did anything wrong. Sometimes my older brothers would tell me to bother her, to see if she would lose her composure, but she was not to be stirred out of her quiet, composed nature.

When our red beans were ready for harvest, we gathered them from the field and brought them into our yard. We spread them out in a twelve-inch layer to dry. After they dried, we beat the beans out of the pods with heavy sticks, harvesting up to two hundred pounds. The girls' job was to help separate the beans from the chaff by scooping up a plateful and blowing off the debris. Then we separated the beans from the tiny stones that had been scooped up with them. Sometimes I interfered with Dada's work by putting my hands over the plate she was using. That slightly frustrated her, but not enough to make it worth my effort. She knew the older brothers were inciting .

me to mischief.

For her quiet spirit and stark, unexciting obedience in a family of many boys, I give Dada my congratulations. I wanted her to stay at our next-door neighbors' home with me when the abicanyi were coming for us, but she had another idea.

Kaka. (KAH-kuh). Full name: Kagabo Kayiranga Jean-Léonard. Nickname: Kaka, which means *brother* in Kinyarwanda. Since I am featured somewhat prominently in my story, I'll move on and say a few things about the two younger siblings I guarded for the first three weeks of the slaughter. Stella and Rousseau occupy a large space in several chapters.

Stella. Full name: Kagabo Umugiraneza Marie-Rosine. Nickname: Stella, Latin for *star* and sometimes mispronounced by older Rwandans as Sitera. Her full nickname is Stella Matutina, which means *Morning Star.* She was born in the early morning. Stella refused to take requests or orders from anyone except our parents and the oldest siblings. She was a "mama's girl" who addressed Maman Paul as Maman, an abbreviation none of the rest of us dared to try. Stella didn't have the foresight to consider the size of our family and see that she might not always be the youngest child. She was annoyed when Rousseau came along.

Rousseau. Full name: Kagabo Sangano Jean-Jacques. Nickname: Rousseau (a French equivalent of *Russell*), after the famous Swiss author, Jean-Jacques Rousseau. This youngest member of our family was obedient and hard-working. He was eager to help us with chores, like the day he offered to help an older cousin cut grass for the cows. Rousseau held one end of a bundle of grass while our cousin swung the machete and struck two of Rousseau's fingers on his right hand. The tip of the index finger was severed, and the finger next to it was cut badly. I was on my way back from a local store when a neighbor boy told me he saw Ingabire walking Rousseau to the hospital, which was ninety minutes away. I sprinted home to find out more.

Rousseau faced surgery with bravery – the kind that was boosted by Ingabire's promise to buy him his favorite soda and muffin afterwards. He was just as brave during the recovery period and beyond, never using the amputation as an excuse to avoid chores. And even though he was righthanded, his penmanship surpassed mine.

Like Stella, Rousseau displayed remarkable courage and self-control when the wicked hunt began and the machete became the weapon of choice against us. He and Stella stood strong to the end, even if they were stricken with fear. We all were.

SHOES

We didn't have public transportation, but we Kagabo boys had tough feet from going barefoot on the rural terrain we walked, ran and climbed. We wore socks only when we wore leather shoes, and we wore leather only when we attended church services, baptisms, funerals, weddings and other formal events. At home we often wore plastic sandals or shoes, especially after washing up in the evening.

Grade schools were for grades one through eight. The one that some of my siblings and I attended was in Kivugiza, forty five minutes away. Papa was the principal and he made the same daily walk we kids made, but not as often as we did. We went to Kivugiza in the morning, came home for lunch, went back in early afternoon, and returned home in late afternoon. That totals to three hours a day and fifteen hours a week. Papa didn't come home for lunch. And since he was principal of another grade school, he walked twenty miles round-trip each week to be there. Nobody in our neighborhood could afford to own a car. Some neighbors had bicycles that they used for transporting harvested crops to market. Papa never owned or rode a bike while I knew him.

No matter the weather, we were not to wear shoes to school. I was embarrassed that the sons of the principal lived by such a silly rule, but I eventually got over that. Papa didn't want us standing out. Some of the other kids had shoes; many did not. One day I showed up in a pair and Papa said, "Why don't you stop that pride of yours?" I kind of understood that I was drawing attention to the fact that our family was better off than most others.

On Sundays, our family wore our finest apparel and walked forty minutes to church. When a church was finally built closer to us, we still walked to the other one because we were so fond of the Muzungu (white) priests. Watching my older brothers assist them as altar boys during Mass made me want to put on a white robe and stand in front of hundreds of admiring people. But by the time I was old enough to qualify, the priests had plenty of help.

Papa didn't mind all the walking. He had walked and biked to the moon and back before I was even born. He and his first wife and their children used to live in his hometown. He taught school there and often rode a bicycle to work. My brothers and sisters walked, just as the other students did. The school cook went on foot too, bringing lunch for Papa. The usual menu was potatoes or rice and sweet potatoes with beans or another vegetable. Sometimes it was a green banana mixed with beans. That saved Papa the round-trip home at midday.

There were no telephones in the villages at that time, nor while I was growing up. When emergencies arose before I came along, the villages sometimes used a communications technology that was faster than walking. They sent important messages by stepping outside their homes and yelling to a neighbor. That neighbor would yell the message to the next house, and so on, until the news reached its destination. That's how my five oldest siblings learned that their mother died at the hospital after giving birth to our brother Ingabire.

Papa's close friend Jean-Léonard was my godfather and the man I was named after. He didn't walk any more than he had to; he owned a car. He also lived near my elementary school. My father used to send me on foot to spend a couple of weeks with him during holidays and summertime. I got to play soccer with schoolmates who lived by him. Life was extra good at Jean-Léonard's place. I didn't have any chores, and I was served an omelette, bread and fabulous tea for breakfast.

Jean-Léonard had what we called Muzungu cows, the modernized kind that ate formulated feed and produced much more milk than traditional Rwandan cows. The Muzungu breed were never taken outside to graze; our climate was not good for them. But they were good for Jean-Léonard's bank account, which is why he had more than bare feet and a bike for transportation.

Long before I was given my godfather's name, before I was conceived, other abicanyi came after my father, his wife and my older siblings. Thanks to a friend's warning, Papa and my brothers were able to run away while the twins and their mother hid safely in the bushes. The abicanyi searched the house and burned it down. When darkness fell, Jolie, Polie and their mom walked for more than an hour to a safe place. Papa gathered the family together again and took them to another good friend, the Hutu governor of the Northern Kigali region. They lived with the governor and his wife for several months and then returned home and built another house. Papa knew more trouble was certain. He requested and received a transfer to teach closer to Kigali, where he felt the family would be safer.

Large plots of ground were hard to find near the capital city, but Papa wanted plenty of acreage to raise his growing family. He found such an arrangement in the countryside, where land was affordable. He built a four-bedroom house and prepared the ground for farming. Later, he hired a Hutu carpenter friend to help add another bedroom and a family room where Papa gathered us every night for bedtime prayers. A simpler house was built across from the first one. Papa's finances allowed it to have three bedrooms and a storage area, all with outside walls of clay and floors. That house is where we younger kids and Papa's mother, Mama Volks, slept.

Mama Volks lived with us until she died. She was 86, I was eight. It was my first experience with death in the family, a very sad time. I loved her and I enjoyed tending to her needs during the last few years of her failing health, when she couldn't walk anymore. She used to ask me to bring her a small burning stick from the oven where a meal was cooking, so she could light the tobacco in her pipe.

Papa's choice of land put us a long way from school. It was the reason I walked three hours a day to get an education. And the countryside was hard on feet. You had to beware of rocks, bushes, thorns and poisonous snakes. The snakes lived in the bushes but sometimes came out on a sunny day to lie in an open area and make vitamin D. An open space above a window allowed one of them to enter our house one day. Somebody grabbed a big stick and killed it before the five-foot viper could hide among our possessions. We would rather walk through the countryside and take our risks than try to hunt down a poisonous snake that could strike at will from an unlimited number of dark spaces. We'd have a hard time going to sleep if we knew a snake was in the house and could slither up our beds, in between the sheets, and onto our skin.

Sometimes I wore plastic shoes when I played soccer in the neighborhood against other kids who wore shoes, but of course I never wore shoes to school. Students who did would sometimes kick at the ball and end up connecting with my foot or shin, and I'd live with swelling for a couple of days. Kicking the ball simultaneously against an opponent who was in shoes was more hazardous. If you played shoeless, you learned to strike with maximum speed and accuracy.

Small rocks in the packed, clay surfaces we played on could be equally dangerous when you were chasing the ball or navigating it through your opponents. One day I very badly wanted to go with my older siblings to a place I can't recall. They wouldn't let me join them, so I wished them a bad time and went to play soccer with some friends. During the game, I stubbed my big toe on a rock in the ground and almost ripped off the entire nail. The blood loss and the wound were gruesome, but the worst part was when Mama Paul took a pair of scissors and clipped the mere thread of tissue that held the nail. She washed my toe with hydrogen peroxide and wrapped it in gauze.

In the privacy of my heart, I accepted the injury as God's judgment for wishing a bad time on my older siblings. I was unable to play soccer for more than a month of terribly long days. Once my foot was back to normal, my life was too.

SORTING THE SNAKES

They started sorting my class out when I was in third grade. The teacher said, "Hutus stand on that side of the room." They all stood. The teacher counted twenty-four. Then the teacher said, "Tutsis stand on this side of the room." I stood up with four others. Twenty-four of *them*, five of us. To me it was an uninteresting task assigned to the teacher. On the other hand, it was the way many of us discovered, vaguely, that we were something besides Rwandans. We did not yet understand that the classroom was a close approximation of the national population: for every Tutsi, there were six of *them*.

The sorting was never discussed in the Kagabo home. We somehow knew that discussing people-group distinctions was strictly prohibited. Even as principal, Papa couldn't do anything about the increasing discrimination against Tutsis. His school district's administrator was a Hutu woman married to a high-ranking soldier in the government. Papa's administrator was good to him, however. She gave him a job during a time when it was very difficult for Tutsis to find employment. He in turn invited her more than once to dinner at our house, probably to stay on her good side, if at all possible.

Deep division between Tutsis and Hutus began when foreigners ruled our country during the last part of the 1800s until 1962. First the Germans classified and divided us by ethnicity. The Belgians did the same during their rule from 1918 to 1962. They used Tutsis to enforce their colonial system and rewarded many of them with better jobs and schooling. All of this drove a wedge between Rwandans, even though most Tutsis were hardly any better off, or were no better off, than their Hutu neighbors.

The Belgians went a step further by introducing an ID card that separated all Rwandans by ethnic group – Hutu, Tutsi and Twa. Hutus and some Tutsis eventually rebelled against foreign control, and the Belgians pulled out in 1962, leaving the majority Hutu political party in control. The ID card system continued to be used, and with a radical purpose of severe revenge on the previously favored Tutsis. By the time I was born, intermarriage had significantly reduced ethnic differences between many Tutsis and Hutus. Still, all Rwandans seventeen and older were required to carry the ID. The Twa are an indigenous group that makes up one percent of the country's population. I myself never encountered a Twa until after the genocide when I visited a cousin who lived in a town where some Twa families lived. Most of the Twa in our region lived in a more remote village, isolated from the rest of society.

Thirteen years before my third-grade class was sorted, Polie's and Jolie's fifth-grade class was sorted. They didn't know who to stand up with – the Hutus or the Tutsis. So they sat until their teacher told them to go over by the Tutsis and stand with them. Like me, the twins thought nothing of it. But ethnic identity had become a more feverish political issue by 1990, when the girls were high school seniors on different tracks of study at different schools. Polie's class had thirty-five Hutus, three Tutsis and perhaps two students of an obvious Hutu-Tutsi mix. Morning break was over one day and the teacher had not quite returned to the classroom while Polie was talking with the boy who sat behind her. He randomly interjected:

Intambara niba ni wowe nzaheraho nica.

(If there's ever a war, you'll be the first one I kill.)

Polie was terrified but didn't mention the incident to anyone until years later.

The government made life increasingly difficult for Tutsis between 1990 and 1994. Public schools were free, but a Tutsi was not likely to be admitted to one near home. And since most families couldn't afford a private school that might be closer to home, most Tutsis in grades seven to twelve were forced to attend distant boarding schools where their families couldn't see them being mistreated, hazed and sometimes tortured.

Papa refused to send his children to boarding school. They went to private schools that were just as far away as the boarding schools, until Papa's Hutu friend and former classmate, the governor of the Northern Kigali region, found a more favorable location for Papa's work and our schooling.

So I entered third grade at Kivugiza Grade School. As was the custom, students sat in twos at their desks. I didn't pay any attention to Karambizi Kaliza Michelle that year, but in fourth grade I was assigned to share a desk with her and I found her to be a very interesting girl. She had ten sisters; I had four. She had five brothers; I had seven. Counting parents, her family totaled to eighteen, four more than mine. She was the baby, and she was nicknamed Mimi, based on the first two letters of her first name, Michelle.

Karambizi Kaliza Michelle lived in Kivugiza and, like the rest of us, was friends with Hutus and Tutsis alike. One school day in the first half of 1993, in fifth grade, she finished eating lunch at home and decided to go to a friend's house a block or two away. She and her neighbors often did that on lunch break because they lived by the school. Whoever finished eating first would go over to a friend's house and socialize until it was time to return to class.

While Mimi was waiting for her friend to finish, the girl's seven-year-old brother came into the dining area and motioned for Mimi to come to him. When she approached, he said something that alarmed her.

"Let me ask you something. Is your family Tutsi?"

"Yes," said Mimi. "Why?"

"Just let me show you something," he said.

She followed him outside to a small storage building. The boy opened the door and said, "Look. Last night they brought these machetes and they said they're going to kill the Tutsis in this neighborhood." He told Mimi to keep it a secret.

She went back into the house and told her friend, "I'm going on to school. I'll see you there."

This incident bothered Mimi far more that it would have bothered me, because she was aware of a government plan to eliminate Tutsis. Her town's local newspaper kept her nerves on edge by running a regular rumor page that would specify a neighborhood and say, "To all of you Tutsis in that area, Wednesday we're going to come and kill all of you."

When Mimi talked to her parents about it, they told her, "We can't do anything but wait." Like many other Tutsis, they weren't convinced that the government-sponsored harassment was more than hot air. The public radio and television broadcasts were filled with programming that belittled Tutsis. The broadcasts used skits, comedy and far-fetched videos depicting Tutsis as snakes and *inyenzi* – cockroaches – that must be annihilated. Some Tutsis laughed at the broadcasts as utter nonsense. But Mimi sensed that something horrible was underway. She wondered what would happen if the Hutus came and attacked some evening before her father returned from his job at the German embassy.

The stash of machetes gave her the evidence she needed. She waited anxiously for her father to get home so she could tell him what she saw and heard. For months she had been nagging him and asking, "Papa, can we just go to Burundi or Uganda?" These are neighboring countries.

But Mr. Karambizi had lost patience with living in exile. He had fled Hutu violence three times during his sixty-eight years. Whatever he believed in his heart about the newspaper gossip, he insisted that it was nothing more than gossip. "They're not going to kill us off all of a sudden," he said. "They're always saying they're going to kill us. I'm done with worrying about it. I've run from them before. I'm done with running from them. I'm going to die here."

This evening was different, however, because Mimi had undeniable proof that she was freaking out with good reason. Her parents would have to take her seriously. Her father had connections at the embassy, he knew people, he could plan an escape. First, Mimi would tell her mother the secret, as soon as she got home from her job as cook and housekeeper for some Canadians who lived in Rwanda.

As soon as her mama arrived, Mimi unloaded on her. She told about finishing lunch early and about going to her friend's house to wait for her to finish. She told about the little brother who motioned for her to come to him. She told about the machetes in the little storage building and how frightful they were. She told her what the boy said and about heading back to school alone.

"Are you sure?" replied her mother.

"Yes, Mama, I'm sure. I saw them with my own eyes. I heard what he said."

"It's nothing," said her mother.

Mr Karambizi arrived at six thirty, came into the house and settled into his favorite chair. Mimi ran to him and sat on his lap. She told him about the machetes and the plans of the local Interahamwe to kill Tutsis. The Interahamwe was a volunteer political group that helped spread the anti-Tutsi philosophy of the majority Hutu party, the MRND. They had been brainwashed into forming militias when prompted by government leaders and propaganda media. Mimi was concerned that a local militia was preparing an annihilation. A child had said so.

"They're always saying that," he said.

"But I saw a stash of machetes, Papa!"

"No, they just do that to scare us."

"Can we just escape to another country?"

"No. I'm going to die in this country. I will never flee this country. I'm tired of living in exile."

Mimi never went back to her friend's house. They played together at school and in the street, but not at the home where Tutsi-killing blades were supplied to the man who was second in command of the local Interahamwe. Mimi's friend's daddy was in charge of distributing weapons to neighbors who were waiting for a signal.

THE MORNING OF THE SEVENTH

Not everyone in my family was home on April 7, 1994. Damas and Polie lived together in Switzerland, pursuing higher education. He worked as a teacher and she was enrolled in teacher education. Jean-Marie was studying philosophy at a university in the Congo. In Rwanda, the Easter vacation for schools was going strong. Leaticau had left the day before to visit our brother Standard and watch soccer with him. We didn't have a TV at home, and not far from Standard's apartment was a sports bar with a TV showing the African Cup of Nations.

At 5:00 a.m. Thursday, April 7, a Hutu neighbor stood in the dim dawn light and banged on our gate. It was eight feet high, four feet wide, made of corrugated metal, and was about sixty feet from the front of our house. Rurangwa, my mother's fellow teacher and also her principal, pounded on the gate until our cook, who slept on the backside of the house, woke up and let him into the yard. Rurangwa insisted on speaking with my father. The cook went in and woke Papa, who came out and learned that the Rwandan president's airplane had been shot down. The Hutu president was dead. His Hutu rivals had been trying to find a way to get rid of him. They bitterly disagreed with his recent policy changes to show favor to Tutsis living in exile in neighboring countries. Rwandan adults knew that the Tutsi-led rebel army backing the exiles would be blamed for downing the airplane, and that all Rwandan Tutsis would pay in some way, to some extent.

Rurangwa didn't have details of the incident, so, after he left, Papa came back into the house and turned on the radio to see if anyone on it was talking about the situation. The rest of us woke up, and to a very peculiar phenomenon: the disc jockey who was always talking and playing pop music was not making a peep. There was no discussion of the downing of the plane. The only music playing was classical. Outside, we could hear loud gunshots in the distance toward Kigali. Our twin-town of Nyarurama-Kimisange was twenty miles from downtown Kigali, but we could easily hear shooting there. We waited and wondered. More shots followed. Then more. I had no experience with firearms. I wondered if I was hearing the sound of killing. I had a strong feeling our world was about to change forever. That radio station should not be playing nonstop classical music.

With daylight came more gunfire. Inside himself, Papa was trying to determine the level of danger and the implications for the country. He told the hired hand who looked after our cows and goats to gather extra grass feed from the field. My playful older brother, Ingabire, was saying, "Hama hamwe, hama hamwe," meaning, "Stay where you are, stay where you are." He thought a couple of people were having a shootout, and he was cheering them on.

Two cousins were with us. Safari was twenty-two and had lived in our home since he was a young boy. His family lived sixty miles away in Shyorongi. Kidende was my age, twelve, and lived thirty miles away in Kinyinya. He had been at our house for a few days, and I had planned to take a one-hour bus ride with him to his house this morning. I asked Papa if I could still go with Kidende and visit my aunt and uncle and other cousins. Papa said to wait. I didn't think the gunshots should stop us, but he said to wait until things settled down. All day long the shooting went on, and when I realized it wasn't going to stop, I was filled with terror.

The now-assassinated Hutu president had recently enraged his Hutu rivals by negotiating an agreement that allowed Tutsi rebels based in Uganda to station six hundred soldiers in a fenced-in compound in Kigali. The rebels were known as the Rwandan Patriotic Front, or RPF, and we thought they might be exchanging fire with the government. But the earliest shots were probably the president's Hutu rivals killing off prominent Tutsis who worked in the government, moderate Hutu officials, the prime minister and her bodyguards, and other officials who could slow down the malicious agenda they had been publicly broadcasting for several years.

In Mimi's town and throughout Rwanda, the downing of the president's plane was a signal that mayors, the military, and the Interahamwe leaders understood. Now they awaited specific orders. Instructions did not reach all areas of the country at the same time, but in Mimi's neighborhood the Army and Interahamwe were all about punctuality. She heard gunshots and grenades. She asked her father what it was about.

"Coup d'état," he said.

"What is coup d'état?"

"A government overthrow."

"So, what's going to happen?"

"I don't know."

"Are we going to die?"

"No. Maybe me, but not you and the others. Just the men."

Government-controlled radio was telling Tutsis not to go anywhere. "Stay in your houses. Don't go running off to a church." This would make the dirty work easier than hunting down all the victims. Some Tutsis ignored the command and fled to a church.

A local leader of one of the several Hutu political parties liked Mimi's parents. She came to their house and found the family eating around the table. She urged them to run away at once because another family had just been killed and the Karambizi family was third on the list.

All but Mr. Karambizi stood up to leave.

"Can you just go, Papa?" Mimi begged.

"I know I'm not going to survive this," said her papa. "They can come and find me. The rest of you just go!"

They did go, and so did the Hutu man the family employed as a domestic helper. Mr. Karambizi hid himself inside. When the abicanyi came and looked in the windows of the home and saw no one, they went to the next house on the list.

By that time, Mimi's mom and siblings and three hundred other non-Muslims were inside a large, elegant mosque built by Libya's then-Prime Minister Muammar Gaddafi. The Tutsi Muslim in charge of the mosque and its campus held the keys to the structure's many rooms. The Interahamwe with their machetes, and some soldiers with pistols, rifles and grenades, went on wreaking terror on the neighborhoods, double-checking the killing lists, and examining every nook and cranny they could think of. They hadn't thought of the mosque.

The Karambizis' Hutu hired hand meanwhile returned to their house and convinced Mr. Karambizi to leave before the killers came back to conduct a thorough search. The hired hand walked him to the Gaddafi mosque and left him with the undiscovered crowd.

THE MORNING OF THE EIGHTH

At ten o'clock the next morning, a dozen Tutsis came running up to our home under the cover of our banana plantation. We knew most of them. The son of Felesi, one of my father's best friends, was with them. They had come fifteen miles, all the way from Karambizi Mimi's area in the Nyamirambo district of Kigali, attempting to put as much distance as possible between them and the weapons that had just murdered some of their neighbors and family – the machete and the *ntampongano*, a long club designed for bludgeoning Tutsis. It was often made more lethal by driving nails partway into the bulging end of it.

Our visitors were bent in painful exhaustion, gulping for air, sweating, and full of fear. They said my former classmate's father Muvara and our friend Adolphe were dead. They said the abicanyi could be headed our way.

We panicked. Papa instructed us to put on plenty of extra clothing because we were going to run away. The visitors we knew waited for us while the others ran on. I put on a pair of short pants, two pairs of blue jeans, a T-shirt, a long-sleeved shirt and a sweater. And my black, leather shoes. Then I went to Leaticau's bedroom and took my coat from one of the wooden pegs that held larger clothing items that didn't fit in the family closet. My coat was gray, heavy and hoodless. No gloves or hood would be needed, since April was never cold like winter. The coat fit me well and wasn't a hand-me-down. My parents bought it just for me, to keep me warm whenever I might be outside in the cool April nights. It extended below my hips and zipped close.

The sleeves were straight and comfortable. The pockets would go empty to keep me as light as possible. I was already lighter and weak from not eating. Fear of dying killed my appetite.

I had the presence of mind to grab another T-shirt, my favorite, a white one with red stripes that Standard had given me along with a pair of pants for taking good care of his two goats during school breaks and feeding and watering them. He had received them as payment for work.

Jolie and Dada woke Stella up and told her to get dressed. She put on a skirt. When Jolie came back and checked on her, she said, "No! You need to put on pants!" Since nine-year-old Stella didn't own a single pair of pants, Jolie and Dada had her wear the pants I wore for First Communion when I was in second grade. They fit her rather well. After the older sisters had Stella layered for the cool night air, Stella picked out a sweater and put on her jellies – the plastic shoes. Rousseau too was outfitted with a sweater and jellies.

Everyone vacated the house immediately in the opposite direction of the gunshots, running through the fields behind our house and into the bush far beyond. Ma Paul, Papa and my older siblings stayed in front of our family, followed by Kidende, Stella, Rousseau and me. We ran and ran and ran. April was the start of the rainy season, and rain was falling. At last, nearly delirious from running through bushes and mud, and burdened with extra clothing and fear of being caught by the abicanyi, I let my favorite shirt fall from my hand. Too heavy, too heavy. I didn't want to leave it, but I couldn't carry it another step, couldn't carry it another step.

And then, somewhere in the wild, thick vegetation of Rwanda, after half an hour of running and climbing the irregular terrain, someone realized nobody was chasing us. The rain poured harder, briefly. A man named Ruru from a neighborhood called Mumena was drained and petrified and clinging to a couple of bushes on a steep section of ground to keep from dropping off. We stopped running and gathered together for another thirty minutes. Around two o'clock, Papa sent someone back to our neighborhood to see if it was safe for us to return and eat. The scout came back and said we could return safely for the time being. Due to the rain, the killing was probably done for the day, wherever it might be happening. We still couldn't tell. Silently, we went home.

Some of the Nyamirambo group, including Felesi's son, were too scared to come back with us after what they had witnessed in their neighborhood. I never saw them again. Jolie was so terrified by the chase that she decided to take her chances of finding shelter in a Tutsi family's house in a neighborhood twenty miles away. "I am not going to die at home!" Jolie said, "I will die running!"

Nobody was actually chasing any of us, because the abicanyi in Nyamirambo had all they could do to find and eliminate the hundreds of Tutsis who lived there, and that would take at least another five days of hard work. Furthermore, the responsibility for scouring our neighborhood apparently belonged to Papa's Hutu friend, Mr. Habimana, president of the local Interahamwe in a fairly large geographical area. But Rurangwa had set off an alarm in Jolie's head when he came pounding on our gate. She knew about a young Hutu man who proposed to another young Tutsi woman and was rejected. The woman told her mother of the man's interest, and the mother told her that a relationship with him was forbidden. The girl passed the comment on to the Hutu man, and he stabbed her mother to death.

Why had Rurangwa come to the house yesterday morning? Was it really to warn Papa? He and Papa were friends. He used to visit us once in a while. Sometimes I went with my father to Rurangwa's house for a meal prepared by his sister, who made all his meals. But Rurangwa had his eyes on Jolie. He and my oldest brother, Damas, were about the same age and walked to school together as teenagers. Both were grown up now and so was Damas' little sister. Papa must have known that Rurangwa wanted to date Jolie, but the two men would not have discussed it, and Rurangwa most definitely knew that a Tutsi victim would be reluctant to allow a daughter to bring a Hutu man into the family through marriage.

Papa didn't have to tell Jolie. She had lived some of the family history I was shielded from knowing. But I had learned some things by the time I was in sixth grade, and I learned them by listening in on private conversations between my older siblings and their Tutsi friends. They had been sneaking off at night to visit Tutsi soldiers at the RPF's compound in Kigali. That's where Cousin Safari acquired some hand grenades. I clearly understood that a separation between Hutus and Tutsis existed, even if I did not understand the conflict.

The conflict spilled over into romance between Hutus and Tutsis. A Rwandan man who wants to date a woman will typically say something like, "Can we be in love?" Rurangwa asked Jolie and she, not wanting to hurt his feelings, offered a polite rejection. She said she was still growing up. Rurangwa replied,

Utegereje kumera amahembe se?

(So, are you waiting to grow horns?)

Our traditional cattle have very long horns that take a very long time to grow. A Rwandan cow is said to have matured when it starts growing horns. As Jolie's fellow teacher and principal, Rurangwa believed she was plenty mature for a serious relationship. How old did a Tutsi girl have to be before she could say yes to love? How long did a cow's horns have to be before it was of age? The girl was a twenty-three-year-old woman, for heaven's sake.

Jolie knew better than to even mention the brief exchange to Papa. Two years later, she was engaged to a Tutsi during a dowry ceremony at our home. Her fiancé pledged a few cows to our family, just as I gave two cows to the family of the Tutsi woman I took as a wife while writing this book. Now Jolie was running from the machete and the ntampongano and did not want to be caught by the man she rejected. He wouldn't offer to shelter her or any of us. Did he come to our house yesterday to get an idea of our escape plan so he could take revenge by plundering some of our animals and other possessions after we left? There was no turning back for Jolie.

Back at our house, Ma Paul told our cook to prepare us some cassava flour meal with vegetables. He had stayed home because he was Hutu and would not be targeted by the abicanyi. My body was crying for nutrition, but my appetite was gone. I forced myself to eat and drink what little I could, which was almost nothing. Rangira asked me where my favorite shirt was. I told him it had gotten too heavy to carry. He laughed and teased me.

It was time for bed. Papa said it wouldn't be safe to sleep in the house, so the older family members disappeared into the outdoors while we five younger ones – Dada, Stella, Rousseau, Cousin Kidende and I – walked under cover of night to a Tutsi's house about twenty-five minutes away, through the fields and woods behind our house and along a road that ran beside more forests. We only have one word for groups of trees in Kinyarwanda. The forests we walked through and past were eucalyptus groves and avocado orchards that we and our neighbors planted. Eucalyptus wood was harvested for construction and as fuel for cooking and heating.

We sneaked home before daylight and joined up with Rangira, Ingabire, Ma Paul, Papa and Cousin Safari. We remained inside the house all day. In the evening, we took blankets out to our banana plantation and lay down on cushions of banana leaves. I fell asleep for a few minutes and woke up, slept another few minutes and woke up again, all night long. Sometimes, in a little bit of moonlight, I saw Papa standing in the middle of us, holding his rosary and praying. It strengthened me a little and also scared me, because I knew he was there to protect us and I knew he wondered whether he could.

The next morning was April 10. Our cook served us cornmeal cream. I still had no desire for food or drink. Close to lunchtime, Gakuru dropped by. He was Papa's Hutu friend, the town manager Papa helped get elected. Gakuru said he overheard some people saying the Interahamwe was coming to our home to kill us. Papa promptly told us to separate into groups and start seeking places to hide far from our neighborhood. Everyone put on extra clothes and grabbed a jacket or sweater and left the house.

Once we four younger kids were out the door, fourteen-year-old Dada pointed about fifty yards ahead toward our Hutu next-door neighbors' house and told us to stay with them. She said to hide there, since she thought we were too young to run. I asked her to come with us, but she said she would be okay and that she was able to run well and that we were too young to run around the countryside. She said the Hutu extremists would easily catch up with us and kill us out there.

There she left us. It was the last time I saw her or Ma Paul or Papa. We had no time for goodbyes. We were fleeing for our lives.

ON OUR OWN

Houses in our agricultural neighborhood were spaced far apart, and all the neighbors near our home were Hutus. The closest Tutsi family we knew lived three quarters of a mile away. The next closest was another mile out. The Interahamwe was about to get organized for killing the snakes in our town, and once it was given the green light, the Interhamwe became nothing but hordes of abicanyi snowballing into a titanic cast of perpetrators of horror that doomed themselves. Someone would give the leaders the instructions they were waiting for, and then every Hutu man and boy of fighting strength would be expected to participate in the militia or in a supporting role, such as searching for Tutsis, ratting them out, or tricking them into false safety. Women and children took part too. These were our fellow citizens, our friends, our fellow church members. They were our judges, police officers, business owners, doctors, nurses, school principals and teachers. And here we were, four children twelve and under seeking protection at the next-door neighbors' house.

Kidende, Stella, Rousseau and I approached the Nyamurwano residence at a brisk pace around 4:00 p.m. The house was surrounded by a fence with see-through, dilapidated sections in front. Gates are usually left open during the daytime, so we entered by a gate on the left side of the house that led to the back. The family knew we had evacuated our house and that we were on the run. They had been kind neighbors for years, and we hoped they would take pity on us now. The father, who was in his mid-70s and unable to chase people

33

down, was not at home. Rudahunga, his son of forty-seven years, lived next to him with his wife, ten children and mother, whom the father replaced years earlier with a woman only three years older than his son.

Supper was being prepared in the open air between the house and a small utility building when we entered the house. A kettle was elevated by three large stones arranged in triangular formation, leaving room for the burning, dried eucalyptus sticks to boil a common staple of sweet potatoes and beans. Mrs. Nyamurwano tended the kettle while a daughter my age washed dishes. The other daughter was Rangira's age, four years older than I. She was inside the utility building, where the kitchen was and where goats were kept in an adjacent room at night. We said to Mrs. Nyamurwano, "We were told to come here." She invited us to have supper.

The meal was ready in a couple of hours. Since we ate with our hands and not with utensils unless we needed a spoon for soup, our custom was to wash our hands before and after we ate. At home we used soap. Mrs. Nyamurwano served each of us a plate of beans with a sweet potato on top. The way to eat a meal like this is to hold the sweet potato with one hand and scoop the beans with the other. I forced myself to eat the potato and to take a nip of water from one of the coffee cups, which had a handle for your finger and were either green or red plastic, just like ours. Even though I was upset, I felt safe for now. I had no thought of how long we would be sheltered at the neighbors' home. Nor did I give a single thought to retrieving anything from my house. As long as I was with Hutu friends, I wasn't running from danger. Maybe my family would be reunited in the morning or the day after, if I didn't die first.

Darkness was falling. We were still eating when, unknown to us, Cousin Safari and his Tutsi friend, Janvier, walked through my family's yard to see whether any harm had come to our home or animals. All was normal. Next, they came to the Nyamurwano house. Janvier's ID card would have shown that he was Tutsi, but he was mixed. He was one of two children his Tutsi father had by a daughter from Mr. Nyamurwano's first marriage. So, although Janvier had Hutu blood through the Nyamurwano family, his father's bloodline determined Janvier's official ethnicity. Mr. Nyamurwano was his grandfather, but once the genocide reached our neighborhood, Janvier would be a wanted man.

Safari asked what we were doing at the Nyamurwano household. We told him we had done as we were told. After some small talk, he slipped out through the gate on the side of the house, hoping we children wouldn't notice. Janvier left with him. But Safari took a path that went between the neighbors' banana plantation and ours, and Janvier went another way.

Mrs. Nyamurwano advised us to catch up to Safari. She was afraid the Interahamwe would search her home if they didn't find anyone at our house. I went out and saw Safari two hundred feet down the path and called out not too loudly: "Safari! Wait! We're coming with you." Moving quickly on the path between the Nyamurwanos' banana plantation on the left and ours on the right, we walked single-file and silently behind Safari, concealed by the night and the ten-foot-high plants from the Hutu homes that lined the road. We didn't see or hear what happened behind us, but shortly after we left, the abicanyi broke into our home and began carrying off our belongings. Other neighbors emptied our entire house the next day and took our cows, goats and chickens and ate them. They stole the metal roof panels, poured gasoline throughout the house, and set it afire. Then they resumed the manhunt and caught Mr. Nyamurwano's officially Tutsi grandson and put an end to him. They knew that snake was out there somewhere.

RWABUZISONI'S BAR

The path was narrow and mostly straight. Ten minutes ahead, the road we were avoiding would intersect with it. Until then, the road curved wide to our right, around plantations of bananas and other crops. We were safer on the path but we weren't taking anything for granted. Four underaged children were on our way to Rwabuzisoni's Bar. Safari's Tutsi friend Michel managed it. My parents sent me there every once in a while with a kitchen container to buy homemade banana wine when we ran out of our own. Living close to the equator meant that we had three growing seasons in the lowlands. Most of our neighbors made banana beer from their plantations too. Banana wine, banana beer, it was one and the same to us, and making it involved a careful process.

First, we gathered several green bunches of a small type of banana and several green bunches of regular bananas. We dug a ditch about six feet deep, two feet wide, and seven feet long. We lined the bottom and the sides with banana leaves, which are enormous. Then we stacked the bunches in the ditch to a height of three feet. We covered the bananas with banana leaves and pushed the dirt back into the ditch until it was filled. After five days, we removed the dirt and the upper banana leaves and took out the bananas. They were yellow and ripe. They were delicious. Maman Paul let us keep two bunches for eating. The rest were ready for making wine.

We peeled them and threw them into an eight-foot-long trough with many gallons of water and a particular kind of grass for pressing the fruit. This was muscular work left to our hired hand and two other men he found to work with him for the day. They pressed handfuls of the grass into the bananas until they were pasty and partially dissolved in the water. Then the liquid mixture was scooped out and poured into three ten-gallon stoneware crocks that had necks wide enough to stick a clean arm down them and stir the ingredients – after we were finished adding them.

Sorghum grain from our fields was roasted and then ground with a stone against a shallow stone plate twenty-four inches in diameter. The resulting powder was added to the crocks. Then we stirred the whole mixture. If we wanted a sweeter wine, we added less water. Once in a while we added honey as a sweetener, but it was expensive.

The trough was raised on one end to pour the leftovers – grass and all – into a fourth crock, to which more water was added. We stirred it with a clean arm and put a long stem of grass in it to use as a straw. I loved drinking the leftovers this way. They were sweet, fresh and delicious. Banana juice by itself was too sweet for me. The sorghum powder made the difference. But fermenting was obvious after two days, and I didn't like the mixture anymore. In the same amount of time, we ate the two bunches of bananas Maman Paul let us have that were ripened underground, a hundred bananas or more.

We stored the wine in plastic jerry cans – the several-gallon kind we used for fetching water – and poured it in a glass or smaller, ordinary plastic containers to serve it. We occasionally served wine in a dried, hand-carved *calabasse* (a gourd that held a liter or two) and let friends pass it around and share from a straw. This happened during baptism receptions and other parties at home. The wine had to be used within two weeks, before it turned bitter and useless. We shared it with neighbors, we drank modest servings with meals, and sometimes we sold some.

My friends and I never played in the banana plantations, but some kids cut the big leaves off their plants and sledded down hills on them. I never ate a peanut-butter-and-banana sandwich either. Never heard of such a thing. Tonight these plants that were such a serious part of our lives were again helping to save us. The sorghum plants helped too.

Our path finally met the road. On the other side were more plantations and our destination, Rwabuzisoni's Bar, a plain little house surrounded by a six-foot-high fence and a wide, open gate. There was no parking lot, because customers came on foot. The house had two rooms in front. The one on the left had become a storage area. The door of the room on the right was halfway open, giving a dim view of four tables inside, each with two wooden chairs. An oil lamp on one of the tables slightly illuminated the atmosphere with help from another oil lamp on the "office counter" by the back wall. Except for these items, the bar room, which had a maximum capacity of twenty persons, was empty. Michel the attendant sat outside.

No stranger would be expected to know this was a bar. There was no sign, no business name, and at the moment no customers. But the bar was open seven days a week from early afternoon to around nine, a place for men who socialized here after work and on weekends, conducting themselves respectfully with one another. They could order bottled beer imported from France, Nigeria and Germany if they had money to burn, but they predominantly requested homemade banana wine, served in a medium-sized *calabasse* that was the property of the bar. Friends around a table drank from the same sturdy straw, a woody stem of grass that also belonged to the bar. A few other domestically brewed beers were available in bottles.

The law did not prohibit us kids from being there, but the bar was a place for grownups, except for nights like this when we were homeless, on our own, and still alive. We crossed the road and took the short path to the open gate. Safari spoke with Michel and arranged for us to spend the night in the back room, his sleeping quarters. Kidende, Stella, Rousseau and I went straight to bed. Safari and Michel talked for a while, closed up the bar, and went to sleep. Before sunrise, while visibility was poor, Safari would take us to the house of Mr. Habimana, a man we knew and trusted, a man my father hired every time he wanted to expand or improve our house.

Mr. Habimana acquired construction jobs with other people from time to time, and he always appreciated the opportunities Papa gave him to make extra money. Being leader of the Interahamwe was a voluntary position that gave Habimana influence and recognition but no income. Papa paid Habimana to take charge of the construction projects, including hiring his own crew. He was Papa's friend. If he had space to take us in, we'd be safe until our family regrouped and went home. Everybody just needed to stay alive a little longer.

TO MR. HABIMANA'S HOUSE

Cousin Safari woke us before sunrise and to another day of trying to avoid being killed. Rarely do children find themselves in this predicament. We left the bar, opened the gate, took the short path to the dirt road and turned left. Without a word, we walked swiftly and in a cluster. The road went to the left in about a hundred feet and then straightened out. Mr. Habimana's house was fifteen minutes down this road that was lined with Hutu houses spaced by more banana plantations. We were totally exposed. Nobody in our town had a car, so we wouldn't have to hide from any drivers who could honk their horns and call attention to us and wake the neighbors so they could come out and kill us. And nobody would expect pedestrian traffic at this early hour. The only reason to be up now was to avoid being killed. But nobody was pursuing us.

Where were the enemies we were fleeing? Who were they? Whoever they were, I knew they were Hutu. All of us Tutsis were moving farther and farther from our homes, and no Hutus were going with us. Stella knew our lives were in danger, but she didn't understand how ethnicity related to the danger. As the two youngest of our family, she and Rousseau had almost no sense of Tutsi identity, whereas Hutu kids knew they were Hutu long before most of us Tutsi kids knew we were Tutsi. After we were sorted in grade three, more of us started catching on. Standing up with a few other kids across the classroom from a much bigger majority of Hutu classmates makes a big impression on you.

In fact, I now recall that it was in third grade when another Tutsi

41

exhibited a heightened awareness of his identity. He had the second-highest grades in the class. I was third. A Hutu girl was first. We knew she was first, because the government forced the school districts to sort us, and the districts forced the principals, and the teachers forced the students. That first-place girl didn't stand with us few Tutsis, and the second-place boy had a new way to talk about her that never would have occurred to us the year before. He said to me during a soccer game at school, "We can't let a Hutu get better grades than us and place ahead of us." He made it his personal goal to place first in the next two quarters, and he did. I was still third.

My family's physical traits were undeniably Tutsi. A Hutu adult, or a Hutu student who knew that Stella and I were Tutsi could look out their windows and see us on the road to the Habimana home and say, "Tutsis!" And then a teenager or adult might go outside and alert the neighbors by patting his mouth to make a warbling sound and shouting, "Hey, look! I see some Tutsis!" It would happen often during the genocide. The warble was part of our culture. You used it to scare thieves and attackers away when you were in a secluded place of danger. The warble was used as a cry for help or a call to action. We knew the sound. We knew a Hutu could run up close to us on the road and warble until other Hutus followed the noise to where we were and hurt us or ran us out of town.

Hutu extremists had run my family off our property before, when Papa and his first wife lived in Mutoyi, a rural town far from Kigali. He was principal of a grade school and he also taught sixth grade, the oldest students. In characteristic fashion, he was quiet about anything he believed would put us at a disadvantage by making us prejudiced toward Hutus. My older sister Polie mentioned the incident to me when I was thirty-six, and my older brother Jean-Marie gave me the details.

The attack, which I started to explain to you earlier in my story, happened in 1973. Polie and Jolie were five, the youngest of the family at the time. Jean-Marie was seven, and Standard and Damas were in grade school. They lived in a home that Papa and their mother constructed out of recycled building materials, assisted by neighbors with basic skills. It was a basic Rwandan configuration and took three months to build. Like the Nyamurwano home, it included a smaller, separate structure serving both as a kitchen and as a place to keep some farm animals at night. By tradition, Tutsi farmers usually kept cows and Hutu farmers kept goats.

Fifty yards from the house, a huge rock on the hilly side of the yard overlooked the valley and the path that Papa and local students took to school. The rock was thirty feet long and ten feet across, a frequent playground for my siblings and their friends. The surface had enough of an incline that they could sit on a piece of stone and slide down the big rock. They called this skiing.

Hutu neighbors were regular visitors at the Kagabo home. And whenever my family made banana wine, they invited them over and shared it with them. Jean-Marie's best friends were Hutu children.

Because of administrative responsibilities, Papa came home from school later than his children. Jean-Marie, the twins and their mother often gathered on the big rock and watched for him to appear in the distance on his way up the long hill. Papa's mother, whose house was a hundred yards from ours, enjoyed waiting on the big rock too. When Papa reached the yard, he greeted them with no special excitement or demonstration of affection, and asked how the day had gone at home. Then he changed into his farm clothes and milked the cows with the boys' help.

Around 10:00 a.m. on a school day in February 1973, an old man named Petero Ntozi who routinely passed by the house stopped in to speak with Mrs. Kagabo. He said Hutu extremists had started burning Tutsi homes in his area and he was sure they would torch the Kagabo home by the end of the day. In late afternoon, the family assembled on the big rock and looked for Papa, waiting to give him the loathesome warning, waiting to hear his plan of defense. Jean-Marie was in anguish and unable to play or eat.

Papa received the news with little expression and said they would leave at night. His wife dressed Jean-Marie in several layers of clothing and sent him with food and milk to Grandma's house, where he and Grandma tucked themselves into a bush under a big tree. The twins and their mother hid among other bushes. Jean-Marie heard a Hutu neighbor yell, "Hey! There are people outside in the bushes!" Papa, Damas and Standard were already running to the residence of Papa's former classmate, Jean-Damascène Birari, the Hutu governor of the Northern Kigali district (the same Hutu who later arranged for my family to move to a safer area when I was in grade school). Mr. Birari and his Tutsi wife Asterie said they would take Papa and his wife and children in until the violence in Mutoyi calmed down. So

Papa, Damas and Standard went back and brought Jean-Marie, the twins and their mother to the Birari home. They didn't see the house burn.

We can't say how Mr. Birari would have behaved in the genocide, but he and his wife helped my family twenty-one years earlier, hosting them all the way into the summer, when they were able to return safely home. Bouncing back was extra-difficult because, before the attackers had set fire to the house, they stole all the household equipment and supplies, along with all reusable construction parts, such as window frames, shutters, and the corrugated metal that was the roof. For the time being, they weren't massacring the local Tutsis. They were acting on government propaganda to make life so miserable for the Tutsis that they would go away and never come back. But Hutu and Tutsi neighbors helped the Kagabos build a small, temporary house that allowed them to get back on their feet again.

Did Mr. Birari take part in the genocide? What became of him? I recently asked Jean-Marie. He wrote:

Birari died in either 1991 or 1992. Before the genocide of 1994. It could be interesting to know how he politically behaved during the 1973 anti-Tutsi pogroms [in this case, persecution of a helpless ethnic group], in his role as prefect of Kibuye at that time. No one knows how he would have behaved during the genocide. His wife Astérie was a Tutsi. She was also the godmother of [our brother] Damas. Before the starting of the war in 1990, one of their sons, Bideri, had been sent to Uganda for studies. He later joined the Rwandan Patriotic Army, a Tutsi-led rebellion, which fought against the Habyarimana regime, a Hutu-dominated government. Our father had Hutu friends, especially from his birth region and from school. The godfather of Damas was Jean-Damascène Kalinijabo, a Hutu from Rulindo who also was prefect of Kigali and later on Managing Director of the Kabuye sugar industry. My own godfather was Gaspard Cyimana, a Hutu also from Rulindo, the first minister of finance of the Government of

Kayibanda. The godmother of Polie was a Tutsi, the wife of
a Hutu businessman from Rulindo, Mr Gakarama.

Those were the days when some of us were still pulling together in
times of trouble as fellow Rwandans. New days were upon us.
Kidende, Stella, Rousseau and I would be okay while hiding at Mr.
Habimana's house, though, because he was Papa's friend. He had
influence as a neighborhood leader, perhaps hoping to work his way
up to being elected town manager one day and having leadership
over five hundred houses, replacing Papa's friend, Town Manager
Gakuru, when his term was up or he retired. Whether Mr. Habimana
liked it or not, he was going to face the reality of power like he'd
never had before and the responsibility that came with it. He would
be given the authority to oversee the obliteration of Tutsis in his area.
After all, people had been promising for years to kill us. Somebody
had to make sure it happened, no matter how many Hutus and Tutsis
didn't think something so insane could happen on the face of the
earth. Tutsi names and addresses had to be compiled and verified.
Weapons had to be distributed. Hutu soldiers, police and civilian
militias were possessed by an electrifying sense of terror-inducing
power. The green light was slow in coming to Nyamirambo.
Everyone there was about to descend into hell.

"EVERYTHING'S GOING TO BE OKAY"

April 11

The road was still empty when we arrived at Mr. Habimana's property. The fields surrounding his house were a patchwork of beans, cassava roots, corn, sweet potatoes, sorghum and bananas. A high wall, or fence, similar to ours encircled his house, not that he had anything special to protect, not usually. We were a simple civilization with simple possessions, though some of us owned things that other neighbors did not, like the shallow stone plate we used when we ground sorghum grain for making banana beer. We borrowed it from our next-door neighbor every time we harvested bananas to make wine.

We turned onto a path that led thirty yards to Mr. Habimana's gate, which was unlocked, and went around to the back door to avoid the possibility of someone seeing him talking to Tutsis and then later using that information against him or us. However, forty-five-year-old Mr. Habimana was going to die anyway, not the way he later feared when the Tutsi rebel army, the RPF, began bringing the hammer down on the breathtaking scale of traitorous brutality. Even while and even before the abicanyi were exterminating the pesky cockroaches who were their godparents and godchildren, their customers and employees, their classmates and students, the government invented rumors about the Tutsi rebels coming to kill all the Hutus. Better to kill all the Tutsis before they kill you! To varying degrees, most Hutus swallowed the government's propaganda without discussing it with Tutsis. The manufactured fear would later turn out to work in favor of the RPF when hundreds of thousands of abicanyi and hundreds of thousands of their relatives would flee the country at the news that the RPF was near. Few in number, the Tutsi rebels were an irreversible force. General Roméo Dallaire said RPF General Kagame "was possibly one of the greatest practitioners of manoeuver warfare in modern military history" (Shake Hands with the Devil, p. 288). Kagame's rebels would have shot the president of the local Interahamwe on sight, but Mr. Habimana did not give them the chance.

Cousin Safari knocked. Mr. Habimana woke up and came to the door. He brought us inside and took us four kids to a bedroom. Safari spoke with him and then left. Mr. Habimana came into our room and said, "Everything's going to be okay. I will do my best to take care of you."

The house was ordinary. When you entered by the back door, a small master bedroom was on the right and a general storage room on the left. This room was also a pantry and, at night, a goat pen. Beyond these two rooms and on the right was the living room. It was the big room, sixteen feet by eight feet, part of which was taken up by some kind of foldable roof panels stacked against a wall, evidently for one of Mr. Habimana's construction jobs and kept inside to prevent the coveted material from being carried off and sold by thieves who could easily sneak in and out of his fenced yard. Our room was on the left. It presumably was designated for the Habimanas' children, both boys, a three-year-old and a five-year-old, but, as far as I could tell, they slept in their parents' room while we were around.

Twenty-five feet outside the back door, at a diagonal to the left, was the bathroom, an outhouse that could hardly be less ingenius. You went in and closed the door, and then you squatted over an eight-inch hole in the wooden floor. Twenty feet to the right of the bathroom and across from the back door sat a small structure a bit larger than the bathroom, that held firewood, water, and equipment for cooking. Between this structure and the back door was the kitchen, a dusty space situated around three stones, similar to ours, similar to almost everybody's kitchen in our town.

Our room was dark. As you walked in, the only window was to the right, on the front wall. The window was shuttered and screenless, three foot high, five feet long, and we were told not to open it. A vertical space between the wooden shutters was just enough that we could press an eyeball against it and see through parts of the fence and out to the road. Sticks and other vegetation that composed the fence had gotten old and fallen off in some places, leaving much appreciated peepholes to the world beyond the yard.

A twin bed occupied the left side of our room, opposite the wall with the window. The door to the room opened to the left and stopped against a small table at the head of the bed. To the right of the foot of the bed, an oil lamp sat on another small table. In all, the bedroom was eight by nine feet. We agreed that Stella and Rousseau could have the bed. Kidende and I would sleep on blankets on the floor.

We were instructed to keep our door closed and locked with a hook and eye, except when Mr. or Mrs. Habimana said to open it. Mrs. Habimana lit the lamp with a match when she brought our meals. We locked the door behind her, and after eating we turned the lamp off to conserve oil. The room was otherwise dark or darkened. We understood the danger of being discovered by visitors and passers-by. The Habimana boys did not show any curiosity about us. From our room, they were heard but not seen.

One vital provision was added to our room – a plastic bucket for urine. We were permitted to leave the room only at night and only to go to the outhouse to have a bowel movement and to empty the bucket of urine there, our daily chore. Mrs. Habimana said to let her know if we had to have a bowel movement during the day, because someone would have to go outside and make sure nobody saw us.

Back in Kivugiza, where the genocide had started on schedule and was in its fifth day, the Interahamwe was killing and stacking and rounding up more Tutsis every day. But three hundred Tutsis on the killing list were nowhere to be found. The Interahamwe hadn't thought to look where my former classmate Karambizi Mimi was hiding with her neighbors and family. While that multitude of fugitives suffered daily hunger, Kidende, Stella, Rousseau and I were eating two hardy meals a day. Sweet potatoes and beans. It was great to be in the care of the president of the local Interahamwe.

A VERSATILE ROOM AND A PACKED HOUSE

April 13

We peeled off the extra clothing we had put on before running from home, and made ourselves comfortable. Mr. Habimana gave us reading materials to pass the time in the closed-up room. I think they reflected his values down deep. He gave us a Bible, sacred songbooks, and a volume titled *Lives of the Saints*. We took for granted that Mr. Habimana was a good Christian. He sure seemed like he was. He attended church services faithfully, he loved singing in the choir, and now he was taking good care of us. We were highly appreciative and we looked forward to going back home today or tomorrow.

A Tutsi woman we knew came to the house with her son and asked the Habimanas to hide them. The Habimanas refused the request and explained they didn't have room. They did allow the woman and her son to stay until evening, thereby adding several hours to their lifespan. Mrs. Habimana came to our room and told us about the conversation. She said, "We don't want to hide any other people. We're only going to hide you." It didn't sound as though we would be leaving soon after all. We might have to get used to our circumstances.

If four kids were going to be holed up in a little, eight-by-nine-foot room, they might as well be given the most versatile room in the house. Our room became many. At noon, it was a washroom when Mrs. Habimana brought a pitcher of water and a bucket. One of us would pour water over another's hands and let it run into the bucket, until all four sets of hands had gone through the routine. At home we had to use soap, but Mrs. Habimana didn't provide it. Once our hands were washed and wiped dry on our pants, she brought our first meal of the day on a twenty-inch plate and set it on the table with the oil lamp, turning the washroom into a dining room. We grabbed and scooped the food with our fingers, not being accustomed to eating with utensils, except for spoons when Maman Paul made soup. This dining arrangement was not so new to us. We often sat on the floor at home and ate from the same platter while the rest of the family sat at the table in another room and shared a platter.

Sunset came at six o'clock and was followed an hour or two later by supper. Mrs. Habimana brought a match to light the lamp so we could see to wash our hands and eat. The old water stayed with us until morning, when she returned with lunch and new water. We blew out the lamp after supper and lay down and talked ourselves to sleep. We had nothing else to do.

Part of our quarters was a reading room during the daytime. We would take one of Mr. Habimana's books from the other small table and see if anything in the pages might appeal to us. We had just enough light to read. Sunlight filtered by April's clouds supplied a glow around the edges of the window and through the slim space where the shutters were fastened together by a latch that we never touched.

We respected the literature Mr. Habimana loaned us, but we were not in a mood for ancient wisdom or church songs or life applications from the experiences of Saints. We much preferred the observatory and the narrow opening in the window that worked as well as a pinched telescope. We spent a lot of time there, pressing an eye to the shutters and straining for clues that would make sense of our state of affairs.

Our living room was where we made small talk. When I wasn't eating, I was usually lying on the floor, sometimes dabbling in *Lives of the Saints* but more often talking about things that would never matter. School should have been back in session, but we weren't even thinking about it. Kidende and I said we'd take that trip to his house the way we were going to do before the shooting started, and we weren't hearing any more shots, so maybe we could do that next week, at the latest. We said we'd ask my parents for money and buy different kinds of candy and give it to his parents and siblings when we got to his house. Planning the trip made it easier to think about tolerating a week or two of boredom, if necessary.

Our quarters also included an indoor bathroom. Stella moved the pee bucket to a corner when she used it, and we respected her privacy. When we boys used it, we stood and held the bucket with our left hand. When we finished, we covered it with a cloth and pushed it under the bed. And when it was time to go to sleep, we hardly had to move an inch. We rolled over and went to sleep in the safety of our bedroom. Our room was a versatile one indeed, and I was happy to have an appetite again. I couldn't wait for my next meal.

The abicanyi in Kivugiza were certain that Karambizi Mimi and many other Tutsis were hiding nearby. They combed the neighborhood homes again and again until they got lucky and noticed Mohamed the groundskeeper walking outside with two young men, Taratibu and his brother Innocent. Mohamed held the keys to all the doors of all the buildings on the campus, including a medical clinic. He and the brothers had gone to the clinic to find something to feed the children in the mosque. They were weak and hurting from hunger. But the three men had taken a bit too long to get back to the mosque. The abicanyi asked Mohamed what he was doing. He said he was carrying serum to sick children. The abicanyi ordered him to lead several of them to where the children were. Mohamed begged them not to kill anybody in the mosque, the ornate, holy house of prayer. The killers had not considered that Christians and other non-Muslims might be sheltering in an Islamic center, and now they had hit the jackpot! They promised Mohamed they wouldn't harm anyone if the Tutsis hiding inside would give them all the cash they had.

Several abicanyi followed Mohamed into the mosque and remained outside the prayer hall while he stepped inside and let the door lock behind him. After a few minutes of frantic conversation among the snakes on the other side of the enormous wooden doors, the killers began urging the frantic crowd of three hundred to open the door and not to worry, since all they had to do was turn over their cash and they'd be left to themselves. It would be a simple financial transaction.

The Tutsis shouted a request for confirmation of terms. "If we give you money, will you go away and leave us alone?" The attackers said they would. Violence in the mosque was unthinkable to Mohamed. He collected the cash the people were contributing to this lifesaving cause, and then opened the door just enough to put an arm through and hand the money over. Suddenly, the enormous door was pulled wide open. The Interahamwe rushed in with guns aimed, ordering everyone to leave the prayer hall. Several Hutus were in the crowd and were told to stand aside from their Tutsi neighbors. In the commotion, twelve-year-old Karambizi Mimi asked a Hutu woman if she could go home with her and family, and the woman gave her permission.

The crowd was ushered on a long walk to one of the biggest houses in the neighborhood, owned by a Tutsi family that would be crammed into it along with several hundred guests. On the way there, Mimi's father became tired from walking and told the abicanyi they might as well shoot him right there in the road and get it over worth, instead of tiring him out. One of the militia shouted at him to get down on the ground. Mr. Karambizi obeyed and prepared to die. My Tutsi friend, Shema, came by. He was my soccer playmate and classmate. He saw the gun pointed at Mr. Karambizi's head and begged the militia not to shoot. "He's a good man! Please don't shoot him!" he said. "He gives us rides in his car." The abicanyi shouted to Shema, "So, do you want to die in his place, little one? Lie down, lie down!" Shema lay down. Then they put a couple of bullets in the head of Mr. Karambizi's sacrificial lamb.

When the crowd arrived at the big house, all the captives were packed into it, unable to move, in one place, of one mind. Among them were Mohamed and the two brothers, Taratibu and Innocent. The doors were shut. The machetes went wild. Mr. Karambizi saw one of the blades strike his son. The boy's head rolled off and Mr. Karambizi fell backwards. Thinking he was pretending to be dead, the Interahamwe chopped him. He didn't move. They chopped again and still he did not move. So they chopped and chopped until they were certain he would never move again when they were gone and no longer watching. Maybe they chopped him because he had a car and most Hutus didn't – neither did most Tutsis – and because he gave children rides in his car and they loved it, and he had a good job, and the TV and radio said he was trash, and he didn't like living in exile and had come back home even though he and his friends and relatives had been run off their properties three times, and besides all of that, he was Tutsi, he was Tutsi, he was Tutsi! What part of "You're not welcome here" did he not understand?

Part of the corrugated metal roof was unfastened and lifted to pour gasoline on the cockroaches. Grenades were tossed in. Shrapnel. Fire. Mimi managed to bring her injured mother and two sisters out of the house after the abicanyi left the scene to call in an armored vehicle that brought the entire structure down with rockets. A handful of Tutsis had escaped with serious wounds to another house. Mimi went in and asked a teenager whose buttocks had been chopped off if he knew anything about her father's condition. The boy said, "Don't even ask me what happened to your father." With that, he fell to the floor and bled to death.

BLESSED CLARE

April 14

To me, the only interesting thing about *Lives of the Saints* was the index of Saints' names in the back that were in my family too. I skimmed the biographical material and never read an entire entry.

One was of Blessed Clare of Pisa, and one of my sister Dada's names was Claire, as in Marie-Claire. I would have to tell her about this woman the next time I saw her. Clare of Pisa was born in 1362 to Peter Gambacorta, a powerful official of the republic of Pisa or something like that, a place I had never heard of. She was only seven when her dad promised her in marriage to a wealthy guy named Simon de Massa. Even at a very young age, she would slip the betrothal ring off her finger during Mass and tell the Lord above that he was the only one she wanted.

She was sent to her husband's home after she turned twelve, and there she started giving generous portions of household supplies to the poor. That's when the mother-in-law, nice as she was, put her foot down and revoked Clare's access to the supply room. So Clare joined a group of women who conducted a ministry to the sick.

Simon de Massa died when Clare was only fifteen. That made her a very young widow. She chose to stay single and to join a convent of nuns. One day her brother kidnapped her and brought her back home, where she was locked in a dark room, away from friends and everything else. Her father was killed by a mob that had turned against him. They put him to death in the street, along with one of his sons.

Lunch was not served to us on this, our third day at the Habimana home. No pitcher of water to wash before eating. Nothing to hold us over till supper at sunset. We were very hungry and we were surrounded by fields of sustenance. Most people in our town had little or no need to go to a grocery store. We raised our own food and we knew what it took to go from seed in the ground to a meal on the table. We ate a lot of red beans, cornmeal and sweet potatoes, and because my family's farm was not optimal for regular potatoes, we did make some trips to the grocery store for those. Other than that, we and our neighbors were self-sufficient foodwise, eating in the order of our harvests, which were many.

We heard a chopper in the sky that was most likely part of the United Nations' preparation to evacuate its peacekeeping force in Kigali. The troops would stay another week and then make a mad scramble onto planes for their own lives, an indication that countries that had an interest in preventing a nationwide massacre had not quite come to an agreement on how to keep Rwanda from falling into self-destruction. We were not aware of these events, but Kidende said the helicopter might be his dad coming to rescue us, even though we didn't know anybody who owned one.

We thought we would be eating red beans at lunch. We and the Habimanas had bean fields, and beans are easy to keep and to cook. My brothers and cousins and I used to beat the seeds out of the pods with sticks. We gathered a pile of the pods and stood around them, one of us striking the pile, then the second person striking, then the third, then the fourth, round and round until all the pods gave up their seeds. That's the way farm kids learn how hunger is satisfied. You take part in creating the food the cook puts on your plate. We knew there were plenty of fields outside to feed us. We also knew that four hungry children caused extra work for the woman preparing the meals we were eating.

In fact, lots of Tutsis beyond the view of our observatory were scavenging for food every day we spent inside the Habimana house. They were still running and hiding, as we had been only three days earlier. Having been forced out from under their own roofs, they were sometimes in the rain, hiding among wet trees and crops and grass during the day, and in the night too, if they lived that long. They dug with their hands to pull up cassava roots, sweet potatoes, carrots, anything, including things they didn't normally eat, like grass. But rain kept the abicanyi away, which meant Tutsis could sometimes find shelter in a small or large building without being bothered for several hours. The abicanyi didn't want to get wet. They could hunt down the snakes when the weather cleared, preferably the next day, not the same day. Hunting was hard work. A few of them took bows and arrows along, weapons that had long since been retired as ancestral decorations, or at least as an old way of life left behind. A few Tutsis took the decorations along too, adding to their odd arsenal of rocks, sticks grenades, and bows and arrows.

When it wasn't raining, the Hutus made chase. At first, nobody in our town knew what was going on. My older brother Rangira, Cousin Safari, Papa and a few other Tutsis made rounds at night near our property on April 8 and 9. Multitudes of Tutsis were streaming down the road by our farm, coming from Nyarurama, Bwerankoli and Gikondo. It was still safe to fetch water and have conversations with Hutus. Later in the day, someone warned us that a group of Interahamwe were making their way to our home to kill us. Rangira came across Konya, a Hutu store owner who wanted to know who wanted to kill us Tutsis. Konya offered to hide Rangira if that became necessary. It's a good thing Rangira didn't take him up on the offer, because Konya soon turned into a hardened killer.

My family attempted to flee to Gitarama, a district south of Kigali, after Dada sent Kidende, Stella, Rousseau and me to our neighbors. They were joined by many other Tutsis on a route that met a series of roadblocks controlled by Hutus. The guards were still trying to figure out exactly what was going on in the new state of alert, and why the road was being blocked. They let the Tutsis pass. But the Tutsis met a brick wall when they came to the roadblock Mr. Habimana was observing. He and Papa had a private conversation. Then the Tutsis went back to Kimisange, our part of the twin-town of Nyarurama-Kimisange. That's when the Hutus launched several days of attacks in the fields and along the roads, starting at about 9:00 a.m. and lasting up to six hours, as the opportunity availed itself.

Rangira and other Tutsis gathered near the home of a man named Sezibera to discuss a defense against the next raid and where they might escape to, if the raids were allowed to continue. Tutsis were running in almost every direction. Some avoided the paths. Others stayed on them in order to get as far away as they could, and as fast as they could, from wherever they were at the moment. They all spoke of finding refuge in different towns but they had no good current information on which ones were safer or which ones were occupied by the Hutu Army or the RPF.

The Tutsi rebels were on the move, but their whereabouts were not easy for civilians to track. Military intelligence was scant, and the rockets flying through the night between one mountain called Rebero and another called Radar could not be identified as belonging to either the RPF or the Hutu Army. Hundreds of Tutsis took their chances and raced to Radar, the moderately forested mountain so named for the communications tower at the top. They were welcomed on the slopes with open arms by ecstatic Interahamwe and Hutu soldiers who guarded the mountain and could not believe their work had been so simplified, as if by saying, "Hey, Tutsis! What are you waiting for? Don't wander in the dark. Let us help. Come to our hill so we can end this disturbing chapter of your life." The swarm of Tutsi was hacked down right where they stood, right where they had congregated voluntarily, right where they had run for fifteen or more miles for protection under soldiers who wanted to protect them but who were on a hill many miles in another direction.

Sezibera told Rangira and the other Tutsis at Kimisange that he would not leave his cows behind and run away from the abicanyi. He loved his cows. They weren't goats! Both Tutsis and Hutus raise goats for eating. Sezibera's animals were the acclaimed, stunning Watusi breed associated with the Tutsi tradition, just like Nice Cow. They have thin, long legs and are agile creatures on the Rwandan fields. By contrast, they have horns of extraordinary diameter and length that would seem to belong to animals two to four times their size. It is said that the dimensions of the horns help distribute the Watusi's body heat like a radiator so the animal can more easily tolerate the high temperatures of Rwanda. At first glance, these cartoonish cows do not even look like cows to most people, because the horns are so outrageous in every way, including being up to eight feet in length and jutting in the most peculiar fashion, depending on the subvariety of the breed. Individuals among their predecessors were reputed to have horns more than twelve feet long, tip to tip.

Most Rwandans don't have pets. The ones who have cows cherish them. Sezibera was known for treating his well, and the size of his herd was a sign of his wealth: he had ten cows! He was not about to abandon them to Hutus who would only cut them up and eat them like goats and never have another thought about them. Sezibera said he'd stay, come what may, and he kept his word. His cows had been as good to him as he had been to them. Their milk had kept him and his family strong. It had been sold at the market to Tutsis who didn't have cows and to Hutus who wanted milk. I loved the Watusi milk as well as the butter we bought that was made from it and used in cooking. Our cook sautéed onions in the butter, poured the mixture over potatoes that were boiled and drained, and then stirred and served the most delicious dish of modern times.

Sometimes we made our own buttermilk, a simple process of leaving milk to ferment in a big calabasse for a couple of days, then mixing it by shaking vigorously and letting it settle until a thick butter-like layer develops on top. We loved to drink buttermilk while eating sweet potatoes, and it tasted even better than plain milk in that combination. The Watusi milk was unbeatable!

But Sezibera himself *was* beatable, and the abicanyi beat him in his home with the edges of their blades. The government had inflamed the killers with polluted imaginations. And even if they reluctantly joined in the killings at first, their consciences had become more callous with each victim they hacked up. Sezibera was a useless cockroach, no longer a neighbor, no longer a person. Cockroaches are pests that multiply and invade. Nobody should feel badly about hurting a cockroach. Sezibera had a cockroach wife and cockroach kids and ten cows and he was too far from the Nyabarongo River to throw him in and watch him float back to Ethiopia, where the Hutu propaganda machine said Tutsis came from, and he was stupid and he thought he was better than Hutus, so he deserved to feel the justice of the machetes slicing into his milk-fed Tutsi skin!

The attacks ended by 11:00 that morning. An hour or so before that, from my hiding spot in the Habimana home, I heard a group of people talking loudly, a half dozen guys who sounded like Tutsis running from Hutus. They said things like, "Get off the road! Go into the bush!" I went to the observatory and cupped my hands around my eyes. They were carrying a body in what we call an *ingobyi*, or stretcher. It's a long pouch made by hand from grass. You insert long, wooden sticks on each side of the pouch so that you can carry a person who is sick, injured or dead. The man on the ingobyi had indeed loved his Watusis. And he was dead. Sezibera was dead. Two men supported him at the front, the middle and the end of the ingobyi. I could hear Safari's and Langira's voices. The group passed the observatory, going left, toward my home and into the bush, out of my view. Something bad was still going on outside Mr. Habimana's house after all.

Sezibera could have paid for a car to transport him to his grave. The ingobyi was for people who couldn't. Yet here he was being toted off like a poor man, away from his cows, his farm, his home, his livelihood, his wife, his two sons who were my classmates in first and second grade. One had to repeat a grade, and so both boys and I met in the same classroom. They lived less than a mile away from Mr. Habimana, and their father was buried secretly in Mr. Habimana's neighborhood, just out of view of the observatory, off the road, off the beaten path, out there in the bush where nobody could interfere with the honorable disposal of a Tutsi cockroach. Trying to bury a cockroach in plain view of the road would've been the end of all six pallbearers. The abicanyi had cut down a harvest of Tutsis out in the fields and entered Sezibera's house while they were at it. Rangira and the other men found him when they swung by his house after the fighting calmed down. His cattle would be butchered a little later, but the only difference between them and Sezibera was that the abicanyi didn't eat him.

Cousin Safari and his best friend Butera were valiant, even though poorly armed. They encouraged the Tutsi crowds and assigned them tactics for repelling the surges of screaming abicanyi. The Tutsis screamed back at them. Every assault cut and clubbed the Tutsis down. Many died immediately. Many slowly bled to death. Others ran off, leaving fewer to face the Hutus.

Dada and her friend Fifi bolted. They ran and ran and ran, and when Dada could run no more, she said she was going to knock at the door of a man named Gahima and ask for water. Fifi begged her to stay away from the house and keep going. Dada said she was too tired and thirsty to go on without a drink. She thought she would die without a drink. Fifi begged her not to knock on the door. Dada knocked. Gahima let her in and, with a machete, removed the head of Kagabo Umugwaneza Marie-Claire Dada.

Safari, Butera and other men in their twenties and early thirties were the frontline against the Hutu assaults along the road. Safari and Butera carried grenades they'd gotten during visits to the RPF, but these were used up in a hurry. The grenades did have the effect of allowing some Tutsi to escape while the killers left to get reinforcements from Interahamwe in other neighborhoods and from Army soldiers. The Tutsis were gathered together the next morning, waiting for the breakfast the women were preparing, when the abicanyi attacked without gunfire. The Tutsis thought they might be able to hold the Hutus off, but then guns began firing and the Tutsis fled in all directions. The blades and the ntamponango were right behind them, and the number of homicides was staggering. The victims were hacked like bunches of field grass. Down they went. Babies. Toddlers. Mothers. The elderly. The others. Safari was hit by a bullet on the inside of his right forearm, just below the elbow.

DANIEL

Daniel moved to our neighborhood two years before we moved into the Habimana home. He was a very nice man. I passed his house every day on the way to and from school and sometimes saw him sitting in front of his house, which was about ten yards from the path I was on. I heard Daniel was a godly man who liked to pray. I saw him walk to church and back with a Bible in hand.

His son showed symptoms of malaria at school one afternoon, and so a student from his class was sent to my classroom with a request that I walk the boy home, since he lived near me. He was eight years old and feeling weak but able to make the forty-five minute walk. I made sure he got home, and then I took the rest of the afternoon off, since school would have ended by the time I got back.

I never saw Daniel give anybody any trouble. He minded his own business and never stopped by our house to visit my parents or bring his kids over to play with us, but people like Daniel made people like me feel safe. He believed in God, had a sense of right and wrong, and he had heard that a million Tutsis had committed grave violations against the country of Rwanda and its citizens. It's one thing for two or three people to complain about someone, but when the country's leaders and the media are voicing the same complaint, you have to stop and wonder if maybe they're not just complaining but actually saying something you need to consider. It's a very negative thing to call an entire division of intelligent complainers liars.

And also, it's one thing for a few people to cast a bad light on their group by misbehaving, but if a million Tutsis are out of line, then you have to wonder who they think they are to be so nasty to the rest of the country. Maybe they think they're better than everybody else and they're planning to take advantage of society. Something's wrong when so many self-centered people have earned such a bad reputation. Who gets called snakes and cockroaches for living like saints? Good human beings don't go around condemning people and ganging up on them for no good reason.

Daniel' head may have been infected with these thoughts. He might not have had anything against the Tutsis, not really, not exactly, although, like Sezibera's murderers, he may have heard national leaders saying that Tutsis originated in Ethiopia. Those leaders could have been quoting anthropologists or geneticists, for all Daniel knew. He was not a man of high education and he wasn't qualified to question scientific conclusions. If they agreed that the Tutsis should be thrown into the Nyabarongo and Akagera Rivers, as more than a thousand Tutsis would be, so they could float back to where they came from, maybe it was a case of a foreign tribe wearing out its welcome. Many Hutus had a hard time sorting it all out in their heads, but Daniel believed in God and maybe he believed God would make sure that whatever his will for the Tutsis was, it would happen, and perhaps the Hutu government was the hand of God in this case, a way to keep order and to guarantee justice. Daniel was still fairly new to the neighborhood and might not have feared what would happen to him if he refused to participate with the Interahamwe, or what kind of harassment his son might face. Daniel wouldn't get to share in the spoils if he didn't participate, and that could seem so unfair, because a person ought to be rewarded for refraining from evil, not for taking part in it. If he left all the goodies for the evildoers, they'd be rich and he'd be poorer – just for being good.

A horrifying, new thing was unfolding before Daniel' eyes as he held his machete in the air and chased into the bush with the rest of the abicanyi and screamed and chopped at the Tutsis who were falling and running. Cousin Safari and the frontline had fled. My brother Rangira turned around and saw Daniel pursuing him and Papa. Rangira in one direction while Daniel and a pack of other Hutus followed Papa into a field and took him down and chopped him until that arrogant public servant, the dangerous principal of two public grade schools who walked forty-five minutes to work every day and probably thought he was so high and mighty and better than everyone else, and he worked to feed and raise twelve children, and he shared his banana wine with his neighbors, and he was Tutsi! he was Tutsi! he was Tutsi! And Daniel and the other abicanyi chopped him until he was as dead and gone as dead and gone could be, and if he didn't like it, then it was up to him to explain why he and his family were still in Rwanda after he had been given more than enough warning to move out of the country during all the years he was being told he wasn't welcome there.

A neighbor said Daniel had mentioned that he would pick up the Bible again after the Tutsis were exterminated. He had a lot of work ahead of him before he could get back to praising the Lord, at which time he'd work out some kind of deal with the Lord to forget the past. Nobody's perfect.

WALLS

We lost track of time in Mr. Habimana's house, and we were hungrier every day, but I was completely sure that he would soon knock on the door of the room he had loaned us, and we'd unlatch the hook and he'd come in and say, "Okay, kids, let's go. Things are back to normal. I'm going to take you back home." It wasn't happening yet, but at least we weren't hearing the gunshots that used to turn my stomach. We were at peace, even if eating only once a day was becoming more painful.

At midday on one of our first several days at the Habimana residence, six-year-old Rousseau had a heart attack. It turned out not to be anything a sweet potato couldn't fix. He screamed and grabbed his chest and said, "Oh, my heart is hurting me!" Stella opened our door and went out to get Mrs. Habimana. We knew she was in the front yard, because we could hear every move in the house at all times. Stella called out the back door, "Mrs. Habimana!" The woman came running to our room and quickly diagnosed the problem and brought Rousseau a sweet potato. After he ate it, he said he felt just fine, but Stella, Kidende and I began reserving small amounts of our supper each evening to keep the little man from having any more noisy heart attacks. It hurt us to see him in pain, but it could hurt us all if he made that kind of noise at the wrong time. The two plates Mrs. Habimana brought us at each suppertime came in handy for storing leftovers so Rousseau would have something to snack on the next day while waiting for six o'clock. Mice ate the leftovers one night when the top plate was not properly positioned over the other one. We didn't make that mistake again, and we didn't forget the robbers were with us. Watching them scurry at will along the walls of our room in subdued light reminded us to keep Rousseau's extra rations sealed between the plates.

The bed was too far from the window to be in the reading room area. I usually lay on the floor below the space between the shutters, which was about three-sixteenths of an inch wide. There I found enough light for a silent – and, as always, incomplete – reading about people like Saint Alphege. It's hard to remember exactly which Saints I read, but they were people like him. He was born not long before the year 1000. He eventually became archbishop of Canterbury. He was strict at the monastery he directed. He wanted the monks to stay on guard against laziness and the slightest disobedience. He cared a lot about poor people and was so generous that you couldn't find a single beggar in his district.

When the Danes were beating up on England, they laid siege to Canterbury. People tried to get Alphege to flee, but he said he absolutely would not. A massacre followed. All kinds of people, young and old, died by the sword. Alphege went straight to the place of the worst atrocities and asked the Danes to stop. He said they could take their fury out on him instead of on the "poor, innocent victims."

The Danes arrested him and threw him into a dark, lonely room. He was released months later while a strange epidemic had broken out. He helped a lot of sick people get better. But the Danes didn't care. They demanded that he pay them a big wad of money to go free. He told them his country was too poor to come up with that kind of money. So they seized him again and beat him with the bones of cattle. He collapsed when somebody hit him on the head with an axe. That's how he became a martyr, a man of faith who was killed for his faith.

Whatever Mr. Habimana was doing during the day was out of our sight. We heard him in the evening, through the door, the way we heard the children and conversations between him and his wife. We knew Mr. Habimana was busy farming and doing construction. Only four months ago he had completed a big project to add a family room, a large bedroom, and a patio to our home. And what a professional job he did. My parents gave Jolie the bedroom, since she was the oldest child living at home and was working as a teacher. In January, we had her dowry celebration in the new addition. Her wedding date was set for the end of the year. Guests filled the family room and overflowed to the outside seating on the patio and in a tent in the front yard.

You can't burn down a house with walls like the ones our house had or like Mr. Habimana's house had. I watched him and his crew make our walls. They used the slender trunks of our eucalyptus forest to frame the walls. The trunks were straight, about four inches in diameter, and were spaced six inches apart the entire length of each wall. Each trunk was sunk a half foot into the ground. More trunks were nailed across the top of the vertical trunks, and then trunks were nailed horizontally into the vertical ones at six-inch intervals, creating a massive wooden frame, a forest in itself.

The next step was to fill the walls with a mixture of clay soil, beige sand, and a blue-ish cement mix. These ingredients were combined with water into a doughy consistency that was pushed into the spaces between the eucalyptus "two-by-fours." It was a lot of work to make that dough and fill up the frame. After the filler dried, the men made cement and applied a layer of it to both sides of the walls with a trowel. Not everyone could afford a cement coating. It took many fifty-pound bags of cement mix. Nor could everyone afford to paint their walls. As I remember, ours were painted white, and the walls at Mr. Habimana's house were not painted.

Mr. Habimana and his crew finished our addition within three months, and when Stella, Rousseau, Kindende and I left with Safari to go to the bar, the neighbors who destroyed our house could not burn it down. They could loot it. They could remove the windows, doors, and roof and let the rain and sun and animals ruin everything inside, but they could not burn that house down. They could only rip it open, pour gasoline on our possessions and set them on fire. Mr. Habimana had made the walls virtually indestructible. What a beautiful, new sight it was for anyone who respected a simple, functional home that was finally spacious enough to easily accommodate our large family, built by the hands of Hutus, ruined by the hands of Hutus. We gave them all we had and it was not enough. I thought we were going back. Jolie had run off into the bush several days ago, thinking someone was going to murder her, but I assumed she'd be back soon. I wanted to go back home and be with my mom and dad and brothers and sisters. I was just waiting for Mr. Habimana to say when.

JOIYEUSE

I still wasn't thinking about school. I would have guessed that somebody was still going to class and teachers were still teaching. With each passing day, this was less the case. The genocide reached some communities several days later than others, and wherever it arrived, Hutu teachers were charged with the daily, urgent task of helping to wipe out the snakes, while Tutsi teachers went on the run. School staffs were reduced to the point of not being able to teach students. The government's Hutu Power philosophy had long been making it difficult for Tutsis to get jobs and education, so there technically was nothing disruptive about Tutsis being altogether absent from school. It's just that there weren't enough teachers to do the job now. At the same time, Rwandans everywhere had the chance to consider a lesson in human nature, a lesson which, stated in the simplest terms, was about how to tell a good person from a bad person. Or you might say it was a lesson about whether the difference between a good person and a bad person is purely a matter of choosing to "love your neighbor."

The good people looked like the bad people on the outside – Muslims, Protestant Christians, Catholic Christians, other faiths, and men, women and children. Sometimes you could identify them by the weapons in their hands or splashes of blood on their clothing or flecks of Tutsi flesh spattered on their shirts. If they were unarmed and clean, however, you would have to identify them by their behavior. Were they good or bad? It depended on the individual. It could even depend on the day. A Hutu teenager might protect his

Tutsi friend and then go out and hunt down fifty Tutsi relatives and neighbors of that friend. A Hutu woman might hide a Tutsi neighbor and then call in the abicanyi after a day or a week of thinking about the wisdom and the responsibilities of hiding someone indefinitely.

Some individuals, on the other hand, were reminders that people can make decisions that go against the bad choices of the overwhelming majority. These individuals were true to core beliefs of human decency based in their upbringing and the instruction of their faith communities, even when their family and fellow believers chose to hurt the hurting and the endangered or refused to lend a hand to them. Individuals who held true to the high standards they professed before the genocide broke out were sometimes prepared to die for their good behavior. Such was a group of Muslim Hutus walking along a river on the worst school day of Joiyeuse's life.

Joiyeuse was a fifth-grader at her local public school in a town far from mine. She went into hiding when the violence started. Her classmates found her disoriented and weak from hunger and sleepless deprivation. They dragged her into the classroom. Several children held her down on the concrete floor and stretched out one of her arms. Another student lifted the ntampongano, the special club that sometimes was enhanced with nails sticking out of the bulky striking end. This one was enhanced. And when it came down on Joiyeuse's hand the first time, the children shrieked with excitement. But she didn't make a sound, being too weak even to moan. That bothered the children. They thought it must've meant she was evil, and evil people must be beaten. So they pounded her hand again and took turns swinging the big club that was meant to be wielded by strong adults, and they explained to Joiyeuse that she was getting what she deserved, a beating for being too smart for her own good and getting higher grades from their Hutu teacher than they got. She wanted to be first in the class? Okay, this is the price to pay. Take this! and this! and this!

The teacher walked by and encouraged the kids to keep up the good performance, and they did, until Joiyeuse's four fingers had disappeared into teeny unrecognizable fragments of black skin turned red and white and only her thumb was left. Then the children tied her hands behind her back, dragged her outside, stabbed her in the side of her stomach, and threw her into a river. That's when her real friends came by, strangers with convictions stronger than all the Hutu

Power put together in the whole nation of Rwanda. They could have been Catholics, they could have been Hindus, could have been children, women or men. They happened to be Muslim Hutus, and they saw Joiyeuse and kindly pulled her out of the river and treated her terrible wounds. They behaved the way we hope human beings will behave when we need them most. You could tell they were the good ones. You could tell by their deeds. They loved poor Joiyeuse as though she mattered.

REBERO OR RADAR

The RPF and the Hutu Army exchanged rocket fire over our valley between the two mountains we called Rebero and Radar. On Rebero was a zoo my family used to visit. If Papa could afford to take a family of our size, admittance was affordable. The zoo included fascinating replicas of traditional huts of the old Tutsi Kingdom, along with real lions, elephants, monkeys, crocodiles, snakes, exotic birds and other creatures. Tutsi rebels occupied Rebero and were trying to drive the Hutu Army off Radar while the Interahamwe were slaughtering in the valley. Godly Daniel and other abicanyi used up valuable time by making sure Papa and many more victims were unable to get back up and run. It was like the Rwandan game in which one kid chases his friends and each one he touches has to stop and sit down on the ground until he has them all – if he can get them. The abicanyi were stopping Tutsis by striking them on the head or neck so they could return to finish them off after taking down the rest of their fleeing targets.

But some got away. Rangira, Safari and eight other Tutsis regrouped in a cornfield for a brief meeting about which of the two mountains the RPF was on. Half of the group said the RPF was probably on Radar. Rangira said he would go with them. Safari said no, that would be suicide. Better to go to Rebero. Through the bush and cornfields half of them ran toward Rebero. Rangira didn't know whether he had agreed to a smart decision, but the bullet wound in Safari's antecubital needed attention and Safari thought he would get medical help at Rebero. The men who ran to Radar ran to their death.

Safari's group reached Rebero within thirty minutes. From another corn plantation, they saw dead bodies strewn along the road. These were abicanyi and Hutu Army. Unaware that RPF soldiers were watching from trenches, the five Tutsi refugees moved up the mountain. Some of them carried a sickle, a short-handled tool with a curved blade used along with machetes to cut grass for cattle. Safari's comrades threw their sickles to the ground and all hands were in the air as they approached a gate. The plan was to get close enough to the soldiers to identify them as either Hutu or Tutsi and then run if they were Hutu. As Safari predicted, they were Tutsi. The soldiers demanded ID, but since Rangira was not yet seventeen and did not own an ID card, he stated his name. One of the guards recognized the Kagabo name and said he knew Papa.

The rebels treated Safari's arm but were unable to remove the bullet. They asked Rangira to accompany them on a mission to rescue an eighteen-year-old Tutsi girl who had become the personal prisoner and rape victim of the son of the man who was Kimisange's town manager before Gakuru, the man Papa helped elect. The girl's brother told the RPF about his sister when he arrived a day earlier. This kind of take-and-rape became a common practice of the abicanyi, and the Tutsi rebels were quite interested in doing something about it. Rangira and four other civilians went with them to locate the house where the kidnapped girl was kept, and to find and bring back food for the refugees and soldiers. They were to keep an eye out for cattle. Tutsis usually ate only the older cows that no longer gave milk, but this was no time to be selective. When they could get a cow up the mountain, they cooked it and ate it there. Uncooperative cattle were not worth the risk of exposing the expedition to the enemy. Some cows ran away when the Hutus came through, and some were eaten by the Hutus after returning from their own daytime expeditions.

Ranchers like Sezibera who were very attached to their cows and didn't want to abandon them to the killers were just as reluctant to let their fellow Tutsis eat them. One rancher refused to give even one cow to the hungry people who were trying to survive the several days of massacre in the valley. After the abicanyi came and took that farmer's cows, the Tutsis said to him, "See, you didn't want us to eat the cows, and now the Hutus have taken them."

The rescue team arrived at the Hutu house in Kimisange in the middle of the night. One of the soldiers went around the house without explaining his intention and busted the back door open. Another soldier shot him, and it was the only shot that was fired, because nobody besides the girl was home. She was able to walk on her own after they untied her. The wounded soldier was carried back to the mountain, where he died. He was the one who recognized Rangira's family name at the gate. Rangira considered the irony: a soldier who jeopardized his life in perilous rescues had died in such a clumsy way.

But there was no time for considering it further. More lives were in jeopardy, more rescues must be carried out. Safari and Rangira informed the soldiers that Tutsis could be hiding in the countryside and in certain homes. The RPF returned the next night and rescued Safari's heroic friend Butera and my twenty-year-old brother Ingabire, whose name meant "gift from God." Butera and Ingabire were hiding in the vegetation when they were found. Ingabire enlisted with the rebels and helped conduct more rescues. Butera would have done the same, but he was killed by a rocket fired from Radar while he was still on Rebero. He had gone outside to find food for other refugees, including many with machete wounds. Safari was devastated to lose this good comrade who had fought with him on the frontline in Kimisange and saved lives. Those grateful survivors bitterly mourned Butera's death.

THE PROBLEM WITH DARKNESS

Saint Bernadette had a brother named Jean-Marie, just like I did, except her Jean-Marie was younger and mine was older. This Saint was born Marie Bernarde Soubirous on January 7, 1844, in Lourdes, France, a town near the border with Spain. Family and friends knew her by the nickname, Bernadette. I wonder what my father would have nicknamed her. He nicknamed two of us with repeated syllables, Dada and Kaka. Maybe he would have liked the sound of Bebe or Berber, but Bernadette was Bernadette till the day she died in 1879 at thirty-five years of age. She's known far and wide for her visions of a radiant woman at a cave in Lourdes.

Bernadette didn't do well in academics or religious instruction at school. Her poor performance may have been due in part to her struggle with chronic illness, especially asthma. Her frail condition also may have left her more vulnerable to long-term effects from a cholera outbreak when she was ten. But Bernadette was wise, had an unshakable faith in "the loving God," and was a superb model of obedience and kindness. She was the oldest of four, five, six or nine children, depending on who you ask.

Mr. Soubirous, Bernadette's father, was a miller by trade and was eighteen years older than his wife. Both worked whatever jobs they could to support their family. The year Bernadette was born, her father rented a mill to grind corn into flour and sell it, but the business didn't do well enough to keep the family from sliding into poverty.

One cold day in February when Bernadette was fourteen, she had her first apparition of "the beautiful lady" while going with a sister and friend to gather firewood. The family was living in a small basement that used to be a prison cell. It must have made Bernadette's asthma worse. The room was also poorly lit and had poor air circulation, similar to the Habimanas' spare bedroom, since we had to keep the door and window closed. Fortunately, we didn't have to deal with the dampness of the basement Bernadette lived in, but we did have the constant problem of mice coming into our room to try to nibble on the small amount of food we stored overnight for Rousseau, who depended on it in order to endure until our next meal, twenty-four hours later.

Hutu friends of the Habimanas continued to visit every now and then, never being invited into the house. The seventy-ninth anniversary of the 1915 Armenian genocide came on April 24, about two weeks into our stay. The nation of Turkey has never recognized its ghastly slaughter of 1.5 million – three-fourths – of the Armenian population. On that anniversary a family friend of the Habimanas dropped by. She was Mukamusoni, the eighteen-year-old daughter of the owner of Rwabuzisoni's Bar who was out killing Tutsis.

We were familiar with Mukamusoni. Her parents had asked Maman Paul long ago to be their daughter's godmother. Our mother was pleased to say yes. While Mukamusoni was sitting in the Habimanas' yard, Stella left our room to use the outside bathroom. A Tutsi girl had become a rare sight to Mukamusoni, all the rarer to see one coming out of the house of the head of the local Interahamwe. The girls said hello to each other and Stella went her way and returned to our room.

"Oh, no. You won't believe who I met outside," she said. We immediately feared that Mukamusoni would tell other Hutus and they would come and kill us. Mrs. Habimana scolded us afterwards and told us that we should let her know whenever we needed to use the outhouse so she could make sure no one saw us.

Three or four days later, we heard Mrs Habimana talking to Mr. Habimana when he came home from whatever he was doing after he left home each morning. We knew what was going on inside the house and in parts of the yard too, but we knew little else. The conversation between them on this day caught my full attention.

Somebody had been killed. A family had been killed. Some Interahamwe had been killed. Tutsis had killed them. The Tutsi rebels. In some home. In a home near mine. The Hutus were the ones who had been doing almost all the killing, so this was the kind of news that grabbed the local head of the Interahamwe by the shoulders and rattled his nerves.

The problem was darkness. Tutsi soldiers moved in the night, conducting rescue operations and killing anyone who complicated the goal of leading Tutsis from known locations to rebel-protected camps. Sometimes they encountered Interahamwe armed with sharpened bamboo shoots, sticks, ntamponangos, machetes and other farm tools. They shot these Hutus. Otherwise, with the help of one or more Tutsis who knew where to go, the RPF soldiers proceeded directly to the buildings, homes and outside places where Tutsis were hiding. Once they found them, they led them to an RPF camp, which could took many miles of silent walking, not as the crow flies, but along winding routes past one town after another, past bodies that were cold with death and stinking from decomposition, past homes where abicanyi enjoyed a good night's sleep before getting up and doing another hard day's work of mind-boggling treachery. But if those resting souls inside so much as awakened and showed any curiosity about the rescue operation, their death was swift.

Someone must have escaped to the RPF and told about a Tutsi who was being held in a Hutu home near mine, and either of those people would know of Mr. Habimana's position in the local Interahamwe. The government had gone to considerable lengths to plan an ultra-quick genocide that would discourage the RPF and render its counterattack meaningless. But the Tutsi rebels were entering areas where volunteer Hutu militia could not defend against bullets, and the Hutu Army could not be everywhere at once. It was under vicious attack from strategic points near the capital city. The Interahamwe had to fend for itself when the Hutu Army was fending for itself.

The massacres continued, though, because neither army could be everywhere, and the Hutu extremists were on target for annihilating seventy-five to eighty percent of the Tutsis in Rwanda. An average of eight to ten thousand Tutsis were cut down, stabbed down, shot down, thrown down every single day. The government's goal was to kill one hundred percent of the snakes — minus a slave or a kidnapped child or mistress here and there — and leave no survivors to tell what happened. But someone had survived and escaped and brought the RPF into the neighborhoods that fell under the responsibility of Mr. Habimana's voluntary, unpaid leadership. He was as good as dead. He was a cooked goose. I don't know how many people he personally killed, or if he killed any. I only know that there is no basis for believing that he had no blood on his hands. At the very least, he apparently helped organize and supervise the extermination of Tutsis in his area. We were constantly astonished by the people we used to trust and who turned on us in order to help Habimana fulfill his part of the Hutu Power plan.

Mrs. Habimana had heard the news about the incident from a good source, and she knew as well as the next person that her husband was a marked man and maybe his wife was too. She was frightened that a Hutu family near the Kagabo home had been killed by the RPF in the dark of night. The parents and their children. What might happen to the Habimana boys? The Habimanas never slept at home again. We watched the four of them leave each evening before the problem with darkness could touch them. We watched from the observatory, and I decided to take advantage of the new schedule, as I was tired of being so hungry.

GOATS IN THE PANTRY

The Habimanas' three goats were safe and on leashes in the room that was dedicated to the pantry and general storage. Thieves sometimes took people's animals. Hardly anyone had a pet, but many people had farm animals, and so it was common at night to keep chickens, cows and goats in a part of one's house or in an enclosure near the house. We Kagabos kept our animals between our house and a field in a basic shelter with a fence on one side that kept the cows from wandering out to where they could be stolen more easily. Breaking into the shelter was easy too, if someone wanted to do that, but it happened only once — not counting the times my family was run off our property and everything was hauled away. If we subtract those occasions, which occurred before I was born, only once did anyone break in and kill one of our cows. And since we didn't have pets, we didn't have watchdogs. The trespassers tore a hole in the cow pen and let a calf out, removed its tongue and left the carcass at the edge of our yard. Real thieves would have taken the calf far away and butchered it to sell and eat. These men were sending us a message.

I said our soil wasn't good for regular potatoes and that we bought them at the market. The market was a large building of eight-foot-by-ten-foot stalls with a counter in front of each one where merchants sold their onions, tomatoes, potatoes, cassava root, sorghum, corn, sweet potatoes, bananas, beans, mangos, avocados, milk, butter, and whatever else they made or grew. Our soil didn't do well for tomatoes either, so we bought those at the market or at approved stands along the road that went by the market's entrance. Like Samuel Taylor Coleridge's famous poem, *The Rime of the Ancient Mariner*, and the thirsty sailor surrounded by salt water – "Water, water everywhere and not a drop to drink" – Rousseau, Stella, Kidende and I were getting skinnier every day in a dark room surrounded by fertile fields of food that were within our reach but would be our death if we ventured out of the house and partook. There was only one way around the problem, and I was too hungry to ignore it.

Sitting and lying around a dark, unstimulating room all day every day made each noise outside our walls all the more interesting. The noises contained information that told where things in the house were. We heard goats in the evening, pots and pans in the morning, doors opening and closing, feet stepping to the left, to the right, down the hall, through a door, and noises outside our window. When the Habimanas began leaving the house at dusk to sleep elsewhere, it was time to dig up some sweet potatoes, and I knew exactly where to find them. The daily sounds of plates and cookware as Mrs. Habimana worked in the room that was both pantry and general storage charted a mental path that I would take when night came, not the first night, but the second. I still wasn't sure that we were going to be alone all night. Mrs. Habimana did say, however, "We're not going to spend the night here. So you need to be quiet." By the second night, I understood: we four kids would be completely by ourselves. The house would be ours.

I only stole sweet potatoes three times from the Habimanas' pantry. I was ashamed to behave like a thief, especially in the home of people who were saving our lives and showing genuine concern for us, if in fact we accurately understood their hearts. But hunger is the mother of invention, as the old saying goes, and I knew that somewhere in Mrs. Habimana's pantry was a twelve-quart soup pot of cooked beans and sweet potatoes. Big families cooked almost every day. We three Kagabos and Cousin Kidende had turned a family of four into a family of eight. Cooked beans were good for two or three days, and Mrs. Habimana had been serving them and sweet potatoes again lately. This told me that she had more beans and sweet potatoes ready to go. If she had started a new pot of them, it would be cooled by now, two-thirds full of beans, with about ten sweet taters submerged in them.

This was the time to make my move, while the taters were plenty. I could stick my hand into the beans and find the taters, count them, and decide how many could be taken without being too noticeable. One or two for Kidende and me and Stella to share, and one for Rousseau to work on until supper tomorrow, about twenty hours from now, if I was correctly estimating the time to be ten o'clock. The Habimanas seemed to have been gone for a long time.

I lifted the little hook on our door and stepped into the living room. Total darkness. Pitch black. But we had all walked the route to the outhouse many times by now. We knew the layout. I did not know where the Habimanas kept their oil lamps, but I would not have used them anyway. Darkness was our safety, not our problem. I stepped quietly in my bare feet along the cement floor through the living room and into the hallway, a distance of several steps, feeling for the walls of the short hallway between the Habimanas' bedroom on the left and the pantry/storage room on the right. The moon was full, possibly hidden behind the clouds, but for sure the back door in front of me was invisible in the blackout caused by shuttered windows and the absence of outdoor security lights and the tiny indicator lights of appliances that can make a modern room glow. Even in 1994, all our nights looked like power outages.

I was nervous. I knew the Habimanas were gone, but one of them might return for some reason. We knew by listening that they did not lock the front door when they left. Mr. Habimana could enter the house and bump into me on his way to light an oil lamp before I had a chance to feel my way back to my room. That would be a capital offense. I had to move quickly. I pressed a hand against the pantry door. It opened inside and swung to the left. I felt around for the big soup pot. A step or two in front of me was a table with food supplies. To the left and out of my reach were the three goats, separated from me by supplies and equipment. They were as quiet as I was. Running my fingers over the items to my right, I identified the pot. The lid was off. I stuck my right hand in. Beans! Two-thirds full of beans! Cooked, drained, and dry, with about ten sweet potatoes the size of my fist that had been cooked with them. Mine for the taking. One, two, or three? I had to decide quickly. I put my other hand into the pot and took a sweet potato with each hand. Could I take a third? This was not a messy operation. I was not taking beans. Beans would fall through my fingers, even if I tried to put them in my shirt. Two potatoes would be easy to carry, and like the beans, they were relatively dry, no water dripping off. I took two, left the door the way I found it, almost closed, and then returned to a room of three half-starved children. I allotted one to Rousseau and shared the other with Stella and Kidende. We had to control ourselves and make the two potatoes last. We kept them on the big plate our supper had been brought on, which we kept on the little table by the foot of the bed. We were prepared to hide the plate when Mrs. Habimana came into our room the next day. The time it took to get up and unlatch the door would be enough to hide the plate. Whenever Rousseau needed another bite or two of his sweet potato, he would say he was hungry and we would give him permission. One sweet potato, eaten during the course of twenty-four hours between meals, did the trick.

The Habimanas returned home at ten o'clock each morning. My third raid on the soup pot was followed by a remark that proved Mrs. Habimana knew the difference between a big pot of beans with the ten sweet potatoes she washed and counted and added to the pot, and the number that remained. Loud enough for us to hear, she said, "You know what, I'm going to kill those goats. They're getting into our food." Death was the usual fate of goats, and we didn't want it to be ours. I don't think Mrs. Habimana suspected that I had stolen the potatoes, but it was easier to go hungry after that than to risk being caught for stealing in the home of the president of the local abicanyi. We had already created a burden for him and his wife. We had created an insurmountable burden.

Leonides lived during the reign of Roman Emperor Septimius Severus. He had seven sons, the oldest of whom was the famous scholar, Origen. Leonides was thrown in prison for being a believer in Christ. Origen wrote to his father and urged him not to give in to the threats and torture and the miserable conditions of prison. The government beheaded Leonides and stole all the family's property. They were left in total poverty. People greatly admire Leonides to this day. I'm sure he knew what it was like to be really, really hungry.

KICKED OUT

Mr. Habimana came to our room right after supper on the twenty-first day of our stay. We unhooked the door and opened it. We hadn't seen him face to face for a long time. He held an oil lamp in one hand and a letter in the other. It was written on one side of a half sheet of paper, supposedly from neighbors. He told me to read it.

> Bwana Habimana, twamenye ko uhishe abana ba Kagabo, none turashaka ko ubica cyangwa turaza tubiyicire.

> (Mr. Habimana, we have discovered that you are hiding Kagabo's kids. We want you to kill them. If you don't, we will come and kill them ourselves.)

We were not shocked. Mukamusoni had seen us and we didn't assume she'd be merciful or that it would matter to the abicanyi that my mother was her godmother. Her father, Rwabuzisoni, could comfortably arrange to have us killed. He might even have been the one who wrote the letter to Mr. Habimana.

Mr. Habimana told us, "Obviously, I'm not going to kill you. But I advise you kids to leave this house and go somewhere else." He said Maman Paul was at Aunt Cyoga's home. He either knew or assumed that Aunt Cyoga was alive, since her husband was Hutu. It was the encouragement we needed to go out into the uncertain Rwandan night and make our way through unfamiliar off-road territory. A normal route to Aunt Cyoga's house would have taken us forty-five minutes. To go that way, we would go out Mr. Habimana's front door, turn left and onto a path that led to a road. We would walk the road for about a mile to where it intersected a path on the right, about 100 yards from Rwabuzisoni's bar. There we would pick up a road going south, take it for about a mile to a steep path that went down to the fountain where we fetched water, then we would follow the path up, zigging and zagging until we reached another path that led to Aunt Cyoga's neighborhood. This route, however, was out of the question. It posed a fatal danger.

We had nothing to gather up, except to put back on the extra clothing we wore when we first arrived at the Habimana home. We hadn't acquired any possessions during our three weeks in the dark room. We in fact had less than we started with, because we had lost weight. Mr. Habimana walked us out the back door and past the wall that encircled his home. He advised us to avoid the road and the regular paths. He said to stay in the bush, but in the direction of Aunt Cyoga's house. He pointed. The rest was up to us. We were leaving the safety of his home, except that it wasn't safe anymore and neither was the journey to Aunt Cyoga's house, starting now. Off we went into various kinds of plantations. In less than a mile we found ourselves on a path near a sorghum field. I knew where I was at this point.

Sorghum is a drought-resistant plant used as livestock feed. It grows tall like corn and can also be ground into sweetener or flour. The flour is used for making breakfast porridge, a good source of nutrition for nursing mothers and for families in general. When the sorghum is ready for harvest, the stems are cut two feet from the roots, put in a pile and brought home to remove the grain, which grows at the top of the plant. Several days later, the stems in the ground sprout shorter leaves that the cows love to eat. Mr. Habimana's father, Mucange grew sorghum. He was also part of the crew Habimana hired to do construction at our house. Papa felt comfortable asking Mucange if our cows could graze in his sorghum field. Mucange always said yes, and I would tag along with our hired hand and help lead the cows to the field, learning the lay of the land without knowing that one day the knowledge would be useful.

Then again, I did not know the off-road parts of the plantations. Still, I was the only one of us four kids who had been in these neighborhoods and fields before. On an ordinary day it would have been nice to be outside, but nothing short of being kicked out of our room could have gotten me to leave it. I didn't want to die. And as the hour grew later, the moon grew brighter, beaming down with sixty-two-percent fullness, bestowing vision for finding our way, and vision for the abicanyi to find their prey. A dangerous escape lay ahead, a meandering route through various neighborhoods. More of my family were going to die, and Kidende and I were twelve, Stella was nine, and Rousseau was six. This was the first day of May. Life had just turned a little crazier.

We wandered on and came to another path I recognized. There we encountered an eighteen-year-old Hutu going in the opposite direction. In the bright moonlight, he could see that I was one of Mr. Kagabo's sons, and I could see no indication of a weapon on him. He told us there was a roadblock a short ways ahead and that one of the people manning it was Rurangwa, the grade-school principal my mother worked for, the man who wanted to date Jolie, the man who was my father's friend. Rurangwa knew us personally, and some of us kids went to grades one and two at his school. By giving us information on Rurangwa, the young man on the path was telling me two things. First, he didn't want to kill us. Second, he knew we knew Rurangwa and he must have thought it was exceedingly odd that a school leader was working one of the most feared parts of the genocide – the valve that made people stop and go, or stop and die.

Well before the genocide, we knew that the Hutu paramilitary organization known as Interahamwe was occasionally stopping vehicles and killing drivers and passengers. Their targets included politicians who showed sympathy for Tutsis. The meaning of Interahamwe had now expanded to include bands of civilians who were Tutsi-killers and who often put up their own blockades at will. Roadblocks were a simple way to stop and demand ID from anyone walking, driving or riding on a busy road. If they were Tutsi, they were killed, piled together, and removed later. Many Hutus who weren't carrying their ID but looked Tutsi were killed as well.

The eighteen-year-old asked us where we were going. We said we were going to our aunt's house, about thirty minutes away. We begged him to escort us. He said, "I'm sorry, I can't help you. I'm on night patrol and I have to be at a roadblock." He seemed like a nice Hutu. At least to us. At least at the moment. He had probably been enlisted with the abicanyi for three weeks but he didn't kill us and he didn't start making the eerie warbling sound to draw the abicanyi to us. He had to keep an obligation at the other end of the path where it curved around and met the road we were avoiding. Mr. Habimana had told us to avoid the pathways, and this was why. The boy knew we were Tutsi. He could tell by our facial features and by our fear. He could've had us killed where we stood.

Several minutes later, a twenty-five-year-old Hutu came toward us on the path, on his way to the same roadblock. He wore a big jacket and looked to be empty-handed. He could have had a machete hanging on his beltline, but I couldn't see one. He said, "Where are you kids going?"

"We're going to Esili's house," we said.

"Who is Esili?"

I said he was Cyoga's husband. I used Esili's name because he was Hutu.

The man on the path spoke with an insulting tone. "Who are you? Who are your parents?"

"We are Kagabo's kids," we said.

His face changed. "What? The primary teacher?" We said yes. Then he looked at me, Stella and Rousseau, one by one, then at Kidende. "This kid with the big head is one of you?" The man slid his right hand into a pocket of his jacket, probably to pull out a knife, which many abicanyi carried when they weren't carrying a machete. Kidende didn't resemble us, and his head was either a little bigger than ours or ours were a little smaller. But as soon as the man reached into his pocket, another Hutu approached. The first man turned around and said, "Hi. How ya doing?" While they conversed, the friend expressed no curiosity about us, so I murmured to my sister, brother and cousin, "Let's go!" We walked about a hundred feet into the sorghum, past a row of shrubs, and stood at the edge of another field, one that had been terraced to compensate for the irregular countryside. Grabbing one of Rousseau's hands, I jumped five feet down. Stella and Kidende followed.

We leaned against the terraced dirt wall and wondered what to do next. Then we laid down for a half hour. When I was sure we weren't being followed, I gave a polite order to get up so we could keep walking. But after thinking it over for several steps, I said crossing the street could be dangerous, because we could hear voices that must be coming from roadblocks. We would have to think about this. Four unarmed Tutsi children had just walked away from three Hutus whose job it was to hunt down and kill every Tutsi they could find. Would they even try explaining to their Hutu friends and leaders that Kagabo's kids walked right up to them and then slipped away in the bright dark of night? Outlandish things can happen when angels walk with you. We did not walk alone.

IN THE FIELD

There we lay, in near silence, in the darkness, in the light of the big moon, in foot-high grass and weeds. To our right was a house, the length of a soccer field away. Directly in front of us, at half the distance, was something that had to be either another house or another roadblock. We must stay out of sight. The field would be our miserable bed for several hours. We'd have to be gone before morning. We kept low to the ground and close to each other. We were terrified and silent, except to pray in whispers while mosquitoes screamed in our ears. I said softly,

Nyagasani Mana yacu utuyobore munzira zose tunyuramo kugeza kwa Esili.

(Dear Lord, guide us on every path we take to Aunt Cyoga's house.)

Night was the time to move safely, but terror, the late hour, and conditions outside had exhausted us. We had moved beyond the noise of a previous roadblock, but not far enough from the neighborhood. We were still nervous about the killer who insulted Kidende on the path. He might be hunting us. He might have rounded up more Hutus to comb the bushes and fields until they found us, which wouldn't be very hard. Dogs were few, but it would only take one to sniff us out.

We wanted to close our eyes and get some good, honest rest. The mosquitoes had gotten theirs — twelve hours of it — during the day and were swarming us with boundless energy, drilling into our faces, bent on getting whatever they could get of us before we were killed and our bodies turned cold. They wanted hot blood, red, hot blood! When we brushed them off our ears, they drilled into our cheeks, our foreheads, our necks, our hands. Even five minutes of undisturbed sleep was impossible. The wispy beasts of the field had come for a battle we were not prepared to fight.

Stella and I knew we were close to familiar territory, and Rousseau knew he was with us. All Kidende knew was that he was in a field and close to death. We swatted ourselves delicately hour after hour, our ankles, our arms, every part of us. Stella busied herself by covering her ears to muffle the maddening buzz and smacking at the mosquitoes and scratching the bites. They were finding her skin through my First Communion pants that she was wearing.

Rousseau's composure was steady, but his tiny seven-year-old body was an easier target for the parasites that lusted for the protein in his bloodstream. I was afraid he would break down and cry. We had been so comfortable at Mr. Habimana's house and now we were exposed to the elements of April. I took off my heavy jacket and put it over Rousseau's face and some of the rest of him so he could keep warm and have a better chance of falling asleep. Mosquitoes were, in a way, the least of my worries, though they worried me a great deal. Whenever they came buzzing into my ears or near my face, I tried to slap them away. But they were fast, and more of them were finding us. Like the Hutus, they greatly outnumbered us.

Four children had been sent into such a night. We were lucky it wasn't raining, or maybe we weren't lucky. Rain would've given us a bone-deep chill and maybe colds, but it would have chased away the mosquitoes. While we were sheltered in the Habimana home, we didn't know rain was often falling on Tutsis hiding among bushes and trees, and that the mosquitoes were eating them up when it wasn't raining.

Just the fact that we were exposed in the open air like this was evidence that something was very wrong. It's what health organizations warn against in countries like Rwanda. We were dressed well enough for the temperature, which was almost sixty degrees, but we should be sleeping under mosquito nets or in a house with good windows. The sheer number and appetite of the mosquitoes increased the possibility of getting malaria, a disease that is rare and dreaded in the developed world but which has always been part of life in Rwanda where nine hundred thousand cases a year are reported. Ninety percent of Rwandans are at risk of the disease, and most who get it survive the usual symptoms – fever, tiredness, headaches, vomiting, dizziness and loss of appetite. Symptoms usually take one to four weeks to show up.

Not that we thought about any of that. We didn't. First and foremost was the problem of getting to Aunt Cyoga's alive. Secondly, as scary as malaria sounds to people who aren't accustomed to it, we knew how to survive it. We were also used to doctoring ourselves with plants like umuravumba and umubirizi, treatments that could be collected from any farm in the community and used for less severe sicknesses such as colds, sore throat and upset stomach. The closest health facilities were a clinic about an hour's walk away and a small hospital an hour and a half away. So we usually only went to a doctor for vaccinations as babies and when we had malaria.

Stella had gotten it once, and she would get it again after the genocide. She was much better at catching strep throat, whereas I contracted malaria every two years. The disease hit me harder than it did most kids, and the only cure for me was an injection in the buttocks each morning, noon and evening for at least a week. The nurse who administered the shots was a Hutu who lived near our elementary school. I didn't have the strength to walk back and forth that far when I was sick, so my father arranged for me to stay at the home of one of his best friends, a teacher who lived near the school, until I healed up and had finished my shots.

I liked staying with that teacher's family. I watched my siblings coming and going from home to school, back and forth, and all I had to do was leave the school grounds, turn right and walk through the gate to my temporary family's dwelling. Hot tea, bread and milk would be waiting for me. Then their son and I would find something to do, like play soccer with his friends, if I was feeling strong enough. When it got dark, we went back to my temporary dwelling place, cleaned up and did our homework while waiting for dinner. I thought of my brothers doing their farm chores and mine, making my life all the sweeter. If you're going to have malaria, this was the way to do it.

Kidende slapped his leg. Stella covered her ears. Rousseau rested under the jacket that covered most of him. I swatted at the ghosts that were biting through my shirts. I could hear them, I could feel them, but I could not see them. We needed to agree on a plan for continuing toward Cyoga's. We kept trying to make sense of our surroundings. We used one arm for a pillow and the other for quietly slapping mosquitoes. The ground was moist but soft enough to provide some cushion. I lay on my back the entire time, constantly looking to the left, to the right, in front and behind us for any Hutus who might be breaking into the field. We'd be easy targets.

They would discover us at some point if we stayed, but moving in the moonlight was a gamble. Everything was a gamble. Could Mr. Habimana have alerted Hutus on the first roadblock to meet us on our way from his property? Could others have waited for us near Cyoga's house, since Mr. Habimana had sent us there? He was part of the leadership responsible for clearing out the snakes in Kimisange. How much blood did he have on his hands? Had he killed twenty-five Tutsis? Fifty? A hundred? By staying in the field, we at least avoided the possibility of meeting more Hutus on their way to roadblocks.

Having asked God for guidance, I was given a strange confidence that he was going to protect us. I was also thoroughly frightened. If we encountered killers, the four of us would most likely run for our lives, not necessarily in the same direction. Rousseau and Stella could not outrun machete-swinging Hutus. I myself was determined to run as fast as I could, if attacked. They would have a hard time catching me. I was known as a fast runner even in second grade. That was the year an older student started calling me Ka Voiture, a Toyota minicar. The girl must have seen me running while I played soccer at the school. I outran all my classmates. And no matter who the physical education teacher put against me, I beat them too.

On my way home for lunch some days, walking in the company of peers, I would hear a sing-song voice behind me:

Nakavoitiri k'agatoyota.

(He's a little vehicle, a Toyota minicar.)

I would turn around and see that same girl. Embarrassed by the attention and the singing, I ignored her and walked faster. But soon enough my soccer playmates were calling me Ka Voiture too.

My determination to outrun killers was unrealistic. How could I leave Stella and Rousseau to fight for themselves. I probably would have surrendered and begged for mercy, or maybe I would have tried to grab Rousseau while Kidende grabbed Stella, and we'd try to run to safety together. But that too was unrealistic. I kept it all to myself.

Stella, Kidende and I weighed our options. The first option was to leave while it was still dark. That might give us the chance to reach Aunt Cyoga's home unharmed. But we would have to make our way along a bushy, unfamiliar cross-country route. The bushes seemed safest, though they would be difficult to navigate. Our first challenge would be to exit the field and get back into the bush by passing the roadblock – a deadly risk.

The second option was to wait for daylight and travel the paths and roads. They would be easier to follow, and since we were a long way from our neighborhood, anyone who saw us would probably not recognize us. We would try to blend in with Hutus who were going to the supermarket to buy or sell food. The same path to the supermarket also led to Aunt Cyoga.

The drawbacks to the second option were: (1) We would be attempting to pass the roadblock in clear view of all the Hutus working it; (2) we couldn't be sure the paths didn't have roadblocks; and (3) we had to be out of the field before workers came and found us hiding. They'd show up by 6:00 a.m. with their hoes to work the soil before the sun became too hot to bear. My family and our hired help worked our land the same way.

The more Kidende and Stella and I looked at what we thought was a roadblock, the more we had to explain the shiny top. It looked like a metal roof. The big moon and the first light of dawn convinced us it wasn't a roadblock after all. It was a house. Except, it didn't have a traditional wall around it, as many other houses did, as ours did. A roadblock would not have a wall around it, so maybe it was a roadblock. But a roadblock would not have a metal roof, so maybe it was a house. However, a house could do without a surrounding wall but not without a roof. We decided it was in fact a house and that the time to move was now!

I was a few months short of thirteen. I didn't know whether we had made the right decision. I woke Rousseau up and said a prayer for us all:

Nyagasani Mana yacu utuyobore munzira ducamo kugera kwa
Cyoga, uturinde abicanyi, udufashe tugereyo amahoro.

(Dear Lord, guide us to Cyoga's and protect us from killers and help us reach there safely.)

Then I put my jacket back on and told everyone to follow me. We met with the road at fifty yards. A half mile to the left was the real roadblock where Rurangwa was stationed. Nobody there would be able to see us. I started across the road and was startled by leaves crunching loudly under my feet. Someone in the house on the right was coughing. Even in the lowlands, a hundred forty miles below the equator, the leaves of avocado and umuvumu trees dry quickly after a few days without rain. I told my three fellow travelers to walk slowly, five quiet steps across the dirt road. I expected Hutus to come out of the house and try to chase us down and hack us to pieces. And yet a strange confidence loomed over me. We did not walk alone.

CLOSER TO AUNT CYOGA'S HOUSE

The field across the road was not planted and offered us no protection. We kept going. We were miserable but we didn't complain, didn't talk. We cared only that we were in danger. As long as we kept moving, we should be unknown to the world because almost everyone slept until it was light outside, and it wasn't very light out yet. We moved to the left of the first house we came to, staying in the bush and the banana plantations that separated that house and several other properties we had to navigate while staying somewhat parallel to the road that went near Aunt Cyoga's house. That road and the one we had just crossed intersected far behind us and diverted at a sixty-degree angle, so that we were now directly behind Mr. Habimana's house, though a long way from it. I kept my eyes on the utility poles and wires that towered above everything else. They carried electricity across the countryside, through the neighborhoods and to an occasional store owner who needed and could afford it for refrigeration. Almost everyone made do with candles, oil lamps, firewood and charcoal. Nobody needed an electric furnace in this climate, but refrigerated beverages were a hot item when available.

We were moving toward a path I had taken before to Aunt Cyoga's house. It would be on our left. Killers could be on it, they could be on the road, but we would not easily be spotted from the road while we were in thick, tall vegetation. Dangerous as the paths were, this one meant speed, and speed was everything at this hour. On the other hand, I was guiding our foursome into plantations and terrain that confused me. The road had disappeared. The correct way forward looked like a best guess that might take us anywhere but where we wanted to go. We had to be at Aunt Cyoga's before the neighborhoods woke up and people started looking out their windows and stepping outside for fresh air or walking to work. Around us now were fields of banana plants with their fruit removed, corn, sorghum, sweet potatoes and other crops that we would be harvesting from our own land some time after we hooked up with Maman Paul and the rest of the family and got our hired help back. It would be fabulous to sleep in our own beds under our own roof, eating more than one meal a day.

We were constantly concerned about stepping on a venomous snake or startling other animals in the bush – a fox, a dog and other creatures that the imagination envisions when you're scared and you're walking in dim light. More than ever, being safe and sound was imperative. Malaria was no game either. Unknown to us, the abicanyi were killing Tutsi patients and health care workers in the hospitals and clinics. Visiting a doctor or nurse to be tested for disease and to get medication could be just as dangerous as going untreated. Somebody like me who required an injection at least twice a day when I got malaria would have to remain in the hospital and be a sitting target. Tutsis were going to hospitals to be treated for illnesses and machete wounds, only to face the ntamponango and machete. One patient who went to a hospital after being chopped across his forehead said the casualties there were mounting as local abicanyi kept checking in to kill new arrivals who had survived attacks by other abicanyi.

This was no time for any of us to get sick, and yet we were subjecting ourselves to conditions that make kids sick and get them hurt and keep them from going to school and doing their homework and chores. But we didn't have any homework or chores, and we didn't have any idea of what was going on at school. We knew we were going to see Maman Paul in about thirty minutes, and she would take care of us from then on if we got sick. She and Papa knew the doctors and nurses, and everybody knew Papa. Ma Paul would know where he was and how to contact him and let him know that the four of us were in good shape. Papa and the rest of the family would meet up with us somewhere, maybe at Aunt Cyoga's house or ours. Rangira could tease me some more about being too weak to carry my favorite shirt that Standard gave me, and I would tease Dada and tell her that our next-door neighbor sent us away after only a couple of hours. We might as well have gone with Dada. I could show her a thing or two about running.

We were thirty minutes away from getting back to normal living, normal meals, normal hygeine, normal schedules, normal clothes. We had been in the same clothes for a long time now. Stella was still wearing my First Communion pants, and I had on my own two pairs of jeans. I never did fit well into my older brother's hand-me-downs, including their shoes. By the time I was big enough to wear their clothes, they were worn out. Their shorts and pants had holes in the back and other places and were unfit for public appearance. We Kagabo boys didn't start wearing boxer shorts until we were in elementary school or later, which meant that holey pants would expose me in the most prohibitive way.

Playing soccer on dirt was hard on our clothing and footwear, and our parents couldn't buy us clothes every time we felt we needed more. I had a pair of colorful shorts that I liked and wore almost continuously because I had such a limited wardrobe, especially for around home. But when I needed replacements, Ma Paul bought new clothes for Rousseau and Stella and nothing for me. I let her know I was upset, and she told me they needed new clothes more than I did. Then it was my turn. She bought me shorts and T-shirts, just what I lacked. When I wasn't wearing them, I kept them underneath my bed, folded and safe inside two shoe boxes to be completely certain they didn't get mixed in with my brothers' clothes that were kept in a shared closet.

Rousseau, Stella and I had birthdays coming up during the next few months, but our culture didn't celebrate birthdays and couldn't have afforded the festivities that are typical in other lands. We would not be receiving any happy-birthday items to replace what we had been wearing. Stella was in her jellies, and Rousseau and I were in socks and leather shoes, the way we attended public functions. We were subjecting our footwear to environments in which our parents forbade us to wear them, except when running for our lives. By the time this whole ordeal was over, whoever survived could use a new pair.

Kidende, Rousseau and Stella followed me along the evasive route I had chosen, until we came upon the path I always took to school.

The lay of the land became familiar to me again. We looked both ways, then dashed into the safety of the bush and fields on the other side. I knew where we were. The ground in most places was firm enough to walk on without our shoes sinking in, but one banana plantation had a large wet section we could not avoid. Rousseau stepped into a mudhole and came to a stop. He pulled his foot out, but the shoe did not come with it. We held him steady, searched for the shoe, plucked it out, gave it to him to put back on, and continued walking. A few minutes later, we passed a frightening scene that made us realize we might not find anyone home or alive at Aunt Cyoga's place. The house of her neighbor, Claver, had been destroyed. The roof, doors and windows were missing, and some walls were on the ground.

My First Communion pants had been forced into irreverent service during the past twenty-four days or so. Under ordinary circumstances, it would take a lifetime of carelessness to make them as dirty and abused as there were now. Little did we know that the suit Papa had bought for me to wear to worship with fellow Rwandans had become part of our escape from people we worshiped with, people who had wandered from God in their heart and whom we would never in our wildest imaginations have supposed that they'd put church on hold long enough to pursue us to our death. Not once would I ever think less of God on their account. I would only see the need to do things His way, lest we reduce ourselves to stupid beasts.

Those pants personified the implications of genocidal insanity – the unlimited potential to choose to consume hateful propaganda until you see no reason why certain fellow humans should exist and every reason why you should snuff them out. Maybe Ma Paul would save the pants for Rousseau to wear as a backup pair for work or play. They didn't have any holes in them as far as I could tell. He would eventually get his First Communion suit. It was a big, beautiful deal that involved a special one-on-one appointment with Papa, the man I was expecting to see soon.

The night before Papa took me to get measured for my suit, he told me to get ready after I woke up because he was going to take me to the city market. I could hardly wait for morning! I thought about the big fling every time I woke up in the night. I was going to be treated like royalty. My brothers had talked about Papa taking them to a nice restaurant after they were measured for their suits. Getting measured wasn't the most exciting part; dining out was, and my brothers made it sound pretty glorious. Sometimes, for other reasons, Papa took along my older siblings – one at a time – to Nyamirambo and let them order whatever they wanted at the restaurant. I waited a long, long time for my turn.

And then my turn came. I woke up to rain that would not go away. I feared Papa would cancel our trip, which would be on foot, since we had no public transportation. But the sky cleared and we went to the boutique so I could be fitted. My suit was gray with a pattern of fine lines, and I loved it, but I loved the idea of going to the restaurant even more. We walked across the street and ordered brochettes, the Rwandan answer to, "What is the best shish kebab in the world?" We ordered fries and a pastry we call cake that looks deceptively like a muffin but isn't, and is better than any muffin on the planet. For drink we had Rwandan orange Fanta, the tastiest orange soda ever invented. I sat there living the dream, eating in a restaurant, guest of Papa. It was an unforgettable outing with him. A physician looked me in the eye years later and said, "If you become even half the man your father was, you will be a great man."

And then, on the day of my First Communion, when I was about half Papa's size but not yet half the man, I dressed up in that new suit and my family threw a big party. Ma Paul's supervision guaranteed that it would be one of the grandest days of my life. Relatives and friends came, some with suckers, chocolates and other candy, and this was on top of all the other mouthwatering food and desserts my family prepared for an occasion that turned the spotlight on me. I didn't sleep much the night before, but the treats and attention I received the next day made the restless night unworthy of consideration. It was a lovely day to be a Kagabo.

WAKING MA PAUL

We hooked up with the path to Aunt Cyoga's house after a mile of mostly intentional meandering from Mr. Habimana's home to here. Another five minutes on this zigzag path would get us to our mother. We were hidden from the road by trees and tall grass until, at about 5:00 a.m., the path opened up right across from where Ma Paul was. From there, the path went on to the few other nearby houses and then to a road with another neighborhood.

What a relief it would be to finally see our mother again. I know Kidende was missing his own immediate family, but he was related to me through my mother's side of the family, so he would feel right at home with Ma Paul, his aunt. We stepped off the path and into Aunt Cyoga's front yard, then walked up to her door, since we still had the protection of subdued light. I knocked quietly. Nobody answered. I knocked again, loudly enough to be heard on the inside. No answer. I knocked again and heard someone cough. That was worth the suspense! We'd recognize that cough anywhere as Maman Paul's. The destruction of Claver's house made me understand that our stay at the Habimana residence had sheltered us from a violent reality. If Aunt Cyoga's house had been destroyed or if she and her kids and my mother had been forced to flee, we four kids would have been in serious trouble again. That cough, that one cough blew away all our worries. We were home again, because we were with Ma Paul.

We were dying to wake her or anybody who would let us in before we were discovered and turned over to the abicanyi. The one thing we could always be grateful for was that Mr. Habimana told us where Maman Paul was. But we had to get her or somebody to the door fast.

Nobody responded. They must've been afraid to open at such an early hour. We were afraid too, but we were outside and we looked like Tutsis and we *were* Tutsis and we had a newfound grasp of the actual danger that had turned our world upside down. We went around to the back of the house where we could wait unseen. We sat on the ground in silence. The cuffs of our pants, shoes and socks were wet from walking through the grass on the path, but Aunt Cyoga's ground was dry.

After an hour, we went to the front door again. I knocked and waited.

"Who's there?"

"It's Kaka."

Aunt Cyoga's middle son Mutubazi opened the door. He was not yet eighteen, and he was shocked. "Come in, come in," he said. Aunt Cyoga came into the front room and was shocked too. She took us straight into a bedroom on the left and made us sit down on a twin bed. She sat across from us on another one. Sad but not crying, she asked where we had been and where we were coming from. We wanted to see Maman Paul. Aunt Cyoga said she wasn't there. The disappointment was staggering. Maman Paul wasn't there. She wasn't there. Mr. Habimana had lied to us.

Aunt Cyoga had probably assumed we were dead, and after we told our story to her and her four children, she surely wondered why we weren't dead yet. She said, "I heard that Rangira and Ingabire managed to escape and they're with the RPF. They're the only ones I know of in your immediate family who are still alive." She said she'd heard during the past couple of days that Standard and Leaticau were in harm's way but still alive at Standard's apartment in Kigali. Leaticau had been there since April 6, the day before the genocide started, intending to spend a few days watching international soccer.

All of us kids were quiet. Aunt Cyoga added, "I can tell you that you're not safe here either." The Interahamwe had searched her house a few days earlier and would be returning unannounced to make more checks. They knew she was Tutsi and that she might hide relatives. Her children legally were Hutu since there father was Hutu. The oldest son was twenty-two and took the role of man of the house when his father was gone. He resembled his father, except that his height – six foot nine – was from the Tutsi side: Aunt Cyoga was tall too.

Her husband was not home, nor was he out killing Tutsis, and Aunt Cyoga was not above hiding Tutsis. She thought it best for two of us to stay with her and two of us to go to Standard's place. We might find safety there or we might be killed. It was also entirely possible that we'd be yanked out of Aunt Cyoga's Hutu house and clubbed or hacked to death if any of us stayed. The Interahamwe had searched under the very bed we were sitting on, and they would do it again. We did not want to all die in the same place. Splitting up raised the probability of one or two of us surviving.

"I don't know how long your brothers will survive at the apartment," Aunt Cyoga said. "It's better that a few of you go and check on them."

If we did not go and if the abicanyi did not search Standard's apartment, we would not know that our brothers were okay for now. And if we all went to the apartment, the abicanyi might force us to split up by chasing us, and we'd lose track of each other. Stella and Rousseau could end up on their own in a harsh setting. Kidende and I agreed we would leave for Standard's apartment in the afternoon. We remained in the bedroom at Aunt Cyoga's with curtains closed, enjoyed some cream of sorghum, washed up, and took a long nap.

Aunt Cyoga appointed Mutubazi to escort us in the afternoon. He had opened the door to us in the morning and he would lead us out, without our extra clothing. As the son of a Hutu, Mutubazi faced no apparent danger, and since he wasn't eighteen, none of us would have any ID to show. We would go on the honor system. It was a preposterous idea! Why, for heaven's sake, would the Interahamwe trust a Tutsi woman who was hiding two Tutsi relatives in the same house they had searched thoroughly and would search again, and who was sending a son to escort two Tutsi boys to visit their Tutsi brothers? Only a blind man could miss our Tutsi-ness. That was definite, but preposterous things can happen when the ministers of heaven walk with you. I wasn't favored above anyone else who was or who had been in the crosshairs of the abicanyi. God was not with me more than He was with others. I was only following a confidence that He would lead me through the insane brutality. The genocide was the first time I ever felt a serious need for God, and there was no changing course now. I was sticking to my faith in Him. I would live a life others would not survive to live.

As we stepped out the front door, a hundred Hutu soldiers came running down the path.

STANDARD'S APARTMENT

The long line of soldiers was running past Aunt Cyoga's house, not at it. We were standing in the valley between three embattled positions: Nyamirambo, Rebero and a government-controlled outpost on Mount Kigali, which was a few miles north of Nyamirambo. From that valley, from Cyoga's front door, Kidende and I were witnessing a brief scene of the war that raged beyond the little bubble we four kids had been living in. Periodic glimpses of the conflict were puzzle pieces falling into place. I had seen the dead body being carried on an ingobyi. We saw the written death threat Mr. Habimana brought us. We ran into the Hutus on the path who were out killing Tutsis. We saw Claver's ruined house. We learned that some of my immediate family might be dead and that it was a big surprise that some of us were not dead yet. Now we were seeing soldiers of the genocide for the first time, and they weren't even interested in us. They were trying to get to their camp on Mount Kigali before Tutsi rebels could overtake them. Mutubazi, Kidende and I went back into the house.

We went out again after about forty minutes, Mutubazi in front, then me, then Kidende – two and a half Tutsis. My head was overstuffed with thoughts I could not process in time to absorb their meanings. I was running for my life again. The abicanyi would find me under a bed at Aunt Cyoga's house and chop me up if I stayed there. I left Rousseau and Stella there because Aunt Cyoga believed it to be the safest way to ensure that some of us might survive this guessing game while Kidende and I walked through territory that had more houses than fields on our way to find out whether Leaticau and Standard had been slaughtered. But what would I do if I got there and found them alive and well? What would we all do? Where could we go? We'd be together but we wouldn't want to all die in the same place. So we'd have to split up and run. But we were already split up. None of this made sense, except we had to know about our family. Aunt Cyoga said Ingabire and Rangira were the only ones she knew of who were still alive, and I had just left my little sister and brother with her. On the Interahamwe's next visit to the house, Stella and Rousseau didn't stand a chance. What would happen to me? I could die, except that I believed down deep that God was preserving me. For something. And why do some people suffer terrible brutality and others slip through without a scratch? I might never see Stella and Rousseau again. I might never have another conversation with Leaticau and Standard. Standard was a father figure to me. Losing him would be…incredibly painful. Maman Paul and Papa could be dead. Aunt Cyoga didn't have any news about them. They were probably dead. She'd be shocked to see them alive, just like she was shocked to see us kids alive. This awful gig was supposed to be over when we got to my aunt's house, but there was no guessing about it — a world of terror had broken loose all around my nation. Mr. Habimana lied! He said Ma Paul would be at Aunt Cyoga's but she wasn't. Did he know she was dead? Did he know Papa was dead?

My head was too full of exhaustion, confusion and revelations to follow any particular thought to its dismal conclusion. I was conscious that I was going to Standard's apartment. We spent thirty minutes on the path and the road that led to another path that went to the apartment. We were young, seemingly calm, and unknown in the area, and the neighbors showed us leniency even when we went around the roadblocks.

We had left the agricultural landscape and transitioned into an urban zone when we reached the open gate of a brick wall surrounding four separate dwellings: Standard's apartment, his landlord's big house ninety feet away, and two other apartments, one being under construction. At a quarter after four, I knocked on Standard's door and went in. Cousin Hyacente, from my mother's side of the family, was there too. He shared the rent with Standard. They were both thirty. They and Leaticau were stunned to see us, shocked like we shocked Aunt Cyoga. She didn't say Standard and

Leaticau were dead. She said she didn't know how long they could survive. She didn't say she wondered how long Papa and Maman Paul or Jolie or Dada could survive. She didn't mention them. So I assumed the worst.

"Where are you coming from?" Standard asked.

I said Cyoga had sent us to check on him and Leaticau, and that the Interahamwe was searching her house for Tutsis.

"Do you know anything about everybody else?"

I said our parents had died and that Ingabire and Rangira had escaped to the RPF base.

At six-foot-three, Standard stood out like a sore thumb with the tell-tale facial features and height of a Tutsi. He was trapped. Hyacente didn't have anywhere to hide either. Standard said Kidende and I weren't safe at the apartment. The Interahamwe had come that morning to take Standard, Leaticau and Hyacente to one of the death ditches to kill and dispose of them there, but a hard rain interrupted the plan. When the Interahamwe first entered the apartment, Leaticau was sitting on a bed, listening to a radio station run by the Tutsi rebels in Uganda that provided information on the rebels' progress. Leaticau turned the radio off instantly. The Interahamwe went into the bedroom and asked him if he had been listening to "the cockroaches' station." After Leaticau denied it, the killers took the mattresses and radio and said they'd be back soon.

Mutubazi went home. Just past the wall outside Standard's apartment was a gate that opened to an apartment owned by another landlord and rented to Standard's friends – a Hutu named Kamanzi and his Tutsi wife, Uwera. They had six children. Leaticau, Hyacente and Standard had lately been staying there during the day and coming back to Standard's apartment at night. Standard immediately took Leaticau, Kidende and me to that apartment and arranged for Kidende and me to stay there. Leaticau would return to Standard's place at night, and I would relax where I was, knowing that the abicanyi weren't going to bother a home where a Hutu father lived.

Kamanzi and Uwera gave us a room and said not to go outside except to use the bathroom. They were people of faith and courage, quite glad to help us. For supper, the Hutu-Tutsi family served us rice, beans and cornmeal. The meal did not fill Kidende and me, but it was enough to sustain us. In times past, Kidende and I would not have thought of these new friends as Hutu or Tutsi or some mixture.

We were all Rwandans. But once we had been sorted and labeled and our life was placed in peril on the basis of ethnic origin, we could more fully appreciate the love our friends were offering. However, we were constantly hungry and we looked forward to every meal, eating twice a day now (breakfast wasn't part of our culture), and not in a separate, dark room. Standard and Hyacente ate with us. Standard helped with the costs and also helped to keep the conversations at mealtime centered on lighthearted topics. He did not tell us that a man from Kimisange stopped by his apartment and told him and Leaticau that Papa had been killed.

Sometimes Kidende and I hung out in the living room and talked with the couple's three boys and three girls. The youngest was a two-year-old girl. The oldest was her twenty-year-old sister. The boys were ten, fourteen and eighteen. Standard said we had no other place to stay, so Kidende and I were still taking our situation one day at a time, hoping life would reset the next day, in spite of gunfire in the city.

The oldest daughter was intrigued by my inexplicably frequent blinking and made occasional comments about it. She thought I was funny. She said to me one day, "I think when this whole thing is over, I'm going to take you to an eye doctor and get you some glasses." She wasn't the first to make observations on my habit. Friends and classmates told me, "You sure blink a lot." One of my other aunts had a husband with an eye problem that caused him to blink a lot. His name was Gasimba. So my family called me Gasimba, but I didn't really have an eye problem and my parents never took me to be checked, because they didn't believe my inexplicable blinking was anything to worry about and neither did I.

THE LANDLORD

Standard, Hyacente and Leaticau saw Karegeya the landlord and his brother every day during the first few weeks of the violence. Karegeya's face began to turn angry, bitter, hateful. He looked angrier each time they saw him. He wanted to kill his Tutsi tenants, but he had two sisters in the way. They respected my brothers and Hyacente. One of the sisters, Bebe, liked Hyacente and sometimes cooked food for the guys and brought it to their apartment. Kidende and I helped eat it once or twice.

A day or two after Kidende and I arrived at Standard's apartment, my sister Polie called from Switzerland. She rang the office phone of the apartment compound and asked to speak to Standard. Polie had been tormented by one newscast after another, and all she could was wonder how her family in Rwanda was doing. Standard told her he was extremely worried, that his days were numbered, and that he had barely escaped death the day before. He told how the Interahamwe had come to take him and Leaticau and Hyacente to the death ditch and the rain saved them but the abicanyi said they'd come back later. He said he had learned that a son of Stella's godmother had just been slain near Standard's apartment. Stricken with desperation and grief, Polie said she would call again in a few days to check on Standard. The two exchanged goodbyes and hung up.

On the early, rainy morning of May 7, Bebe came to Standard's apartment and said she overheard her brother saying he was sending the Interahamwe to kill the guys within hours. But the killers didn't come. Bebe came again the next morning with the same message.

This time Standard went next door to Kamanzi's and Uwera's apartment and told me and Kidende to come to his apartment, where he held a meeting with us in his bedroom. He told us the abicanyi were coming to kill him, Leaticau and Hyacente. He said Kidende and I had to leave. Standard was rattled but outwardly calm. He advised us to go to our Aunt Anonciata's house, implying that he knew she was still alive. "I have to stay here," he said. "There's no place to hide." He said he would be caught and killed within mere minutes if he tried to escape.

He took a piece of paper, tore it into six tiny strips, and wrote his bank account number on them. He gave each of us two duplicates to ensure that somebody in the family would be able to get their hands on his hard-earned money when peace was restored. "If you survive, go to the bank and see if you can take the money out of my account," he said. Not a dime of it was ever recovered. It was nice of Standard to think of us, but money was the last thing on our minds. We were trying not to die. No, money was not interesting, not to kids who were used to someone providing for us. Within two months, those little strips of paper would somehow, somewhere be lost forever, the banks would be worthless, the Rwandan economy would be shattered.

Standard then gave Kidende and me each an empty plastic grocery bag so that, instead of looking like we were trying to avoid being killed while walking two miles to Aunt Anonciata's home, we would appear to be going to the supermarket, which we would pass a quarter mile before we got to her place. Standard said goodbye without emotion and sent us out. We were on the move again, doing our best to stay alive again, walking in the open on a road again, because we had no choice. We had slept at three different Hutu homes: Rwabuzisoni's Bar, the Habimana home, and Kamanzi's apartment. All this commotion and I still did not have my mother back. I thought living in a Hutu home for three weeks would be the best protection available. I guess it was for three weeks, but I thought I'd be going home after that. Mr. Habimana didn't defend us. And he lied about my mother. Still, I am grateful to this day that he shielded us from death for a while.

Anyone who thinks Mr. Habimana was probably a good man doesn't understand human nature very well. Anyone who thinks he was totally evil doesn't understand genocide. "Habimana" means "God exists," and Mr. Habimana had a genuine interest in God. The books he loaned us kids, along with the way he treated and spoke to us, tell me he yearned for a supernatural touch on his life. However, he was not prepared to resist the influences that take a person in another direction. It's not enough to want something good; you have to want it really bad.

Mr. Habimana was not involved in the genocide in a "possible" or a "probable" way. He was involved in large-scale brutality. I'm sure he didn't enjoy it. I'm sure he was ashamed. I'm sure he cared about us children and about my parents, and I'm also sure he cared more about his own wellbeing than he did anything else. He was afraid of what could happen to him if he refused to organize the killings and plundering, and especially to resist them. Resistance would have added four Habimanas to the piles and piles of bodies throughout Rwanda. Inaction would have brought him some ridicule and the promise of no promotion to paid public office.

But if I give him a momentary break and look on the bright side, I might find enough goodness in Mr. Habimana to nominate him for sainthood and get him a place in his book, *Lives of the Saints*. It takes imagination, and I'd have to ignore all the people who were killed under his supervision and all the survivors and their families and friends who are not here to dispute the list of good deeds and good character traits that I can attribute to Mr. Habimana. All I want to do is show that genocide is paradoxical by showing that even people who yearn for God or for goodness can make choices that contradict everything they have professed and lived, when terrible propaganda and terrible fear is placed on them. It's a terrifying thing to discover that we are able to do things we were sure we'd never do. If we're honest when we look at others, we see in ourselves the same potential to do good and evil. We all sin. We all fall short, every day. This is why following God is a daily decision, not a Sunday church service, not membership in a certain group.

On Mr. Habimana's behalf, I say the following:

○ He was a conscientious worker. He made our house look better than his, and he made it stronger than his. He earned his pay.

○ He gave Rousseau, Kidende, Stella and me permission to stay at his house on a moment's notice, and his wife fed us the food they grew.

∘ He came up with a gentle way to tell us kids we had to leave his property. He may have written the letter he had me read "from the neighbors" – I don't know – but it served its purpose and it really wasn't a lie. He too was surrounded by abicanyi.

∘ He and his wife were basically running a small orphanage while we were in their home. One meal a day was not out of the ordinary for orphans.

∘ He told us he wasn't going to kill us, and he meant it. He was determined not to have our blood on his hands. We mattered to him.

∘ He must have checked into Cyoga's status for our sake, because he pointed us to her house and seemed to genuinely wish us the best.

∘ He sent us away at night and advised us to stay off paths and roads. These were the smartest safety precautions, in spite of deadly risks.

∘ He kept us for as long as he could without endangering his family and himself. The bar owner's daughter Mukamusoni saw Stella going to the outhouse, and we were well aware of the implications. Even if it were possible to say that the mistake did not endanger Mr. Habimana and his family, it put our lives on the line. We would have been killed shortly.

∘ He didn't acquire other people's possessions by stealing from the dead. At least I did not see or hear him bring anything onto his property.

For his demonstrations of good character, for his generosity in tough economic times, and for taking known risks on our behalf until the end when it would have done us no good for him to try to shield us from the abicanyi, I nominate Mr. Habimana for consideration as a Saint. By my own authority, this preliminary phase confers on him the title, Servant of God, the first of four certified steps toward full-fledged Sainthood. By day he was killer and by God's plan he was servant to a story that more than a million dead and thousands of survivors could not tell. Mr. Habimana was like an angel on my path, but he was neither angel nor saint. He was a man torn by a desire to do good and a stronger desire to save his own skin. But he could not save it from the mosquitoes that flourished in the rainy season and filled the open air where Hutus hunted Tutsis. Habimana would die at home of high fever and vomiting, not far from a hospital that ordinarily treated malaria but was now overloaded with casualties of genocide and was running low on medicines and staff. If you weren't treated for malaria, you died. Habimana would expire at home instead of in a refugee camp across the Rwandan border where medications were even more scarce and people were crowded together with vomiting, defecating, perishing family and neighbors. Before Habimana breathed his last, the machete alone would take the lives of hundreds of thousands more victims from towns all over Rwanda as local Interahamwe leaders helped execute the most efficient large-scale slaughter in history.

Kidende and I and our empty plastic bags were at the edge of the supermarket within fifteen minutes. It was on our left. The road was paved here and had wide sidewalks on both sides of this busy commercial area. Vendors were setting up their booths inside the big store. A roadblock a hundred feet in front of us was slowing the vehicular and pedestrian traffic and making us less distinct in the compressed crowd. Multiple guards were stationed at each end of the barricade. They checked ID and evaluated physical characteristics. Bodies were normally piled beside the roadblocks, but the traffic congestion and my concentration prevented me from seeing them.

I knew this route. Kidende and I stepped onto the sidewalk and kept walking. Cars were coming and going, people were crossing the road in both directions, going in and out of the supermarket. Its broad entrance was only thirty feet from the road and merged with everything into a single hub of activity. There was no time for talking anything over. We had to move through the crowd at a normal pace, looking like everybody else – busy, on task, unconcerned with anyone else's business. A small boutique sat between us and the roadblock, right where a guard might have made a comfortable turn of his head and noticed us and added us to the body piles.

LUNCH AT AUNT ANONCIATA'S HOUSE

The sidewalk ended in another thirty feet. We stepped onto the road again and into the coming and going of morning pedestrian traffic. We would have to carry our empty shopping bags three more city blocks before we'd be at the home of Anonciata, my aunt and Kidende's. Standard, Hyacente and Leaticau would have been pulled aside and killed if they had been with us. And then Kidende and I would've been killed too, because the abicanyi would have looked at us and said, "Obviously they're Tutsis, and obviously they're trying to escape." All in all, it would be a five-in-one bargain for the abicanyi. Of course, we never would have made it past the roadblock, not even if we had all been carrying an empty plastic shopping bag. We'd be on the body piles or hauled away to one of the ditches by enthusiastic stoners and clubbers.

We were three city blocks away from Aunt Anonciata. The killers we met on the path after we left Saint Mr. Habimana's property knew I was Tutsi if I were Principal Kagabo's kid. I looked like Papa, and Stella closely resembled me. Rousseau was darker and looked more like other family members. Just as our friends and neighbors had betrayed us, even strangers considered it a duty and a privilege to detain us and verify our ancestry and to cut our dreams and aspirations short with their blades. I never told anyone, but a Hutu stranger about fifty years old stopped me on my way home when I was seven. As I was about to walk past him on a path through the plantations, he grabbed my arm and demanded,

Uri uwo kwande sha?

(Whose home do you belong to? or, Who is your father?)

I broke loose and ran like the wind. I kept the matter to myself out of fear that I'd get in trouble if my parents learned about it, even though I hadn't done anything wrong.

What would Aunt Anonciata do with us after we got to her house? How long would we be there? Would she take care of us? Could she protect us? She was a widow and a Tutsi. How many of my family would be alive by afternoon? How many by evening? I was inferring that my parents were dead, and I told Standard and Hyacente and Leaticau they were dead, but I didn't actually know they were. It seemed like they must be. They probably were. But maybe not. I was kind of assuming Kidende would still be around once the violence stopped. His father, brother of Aunt Anonciata, would soon be killed, and Anonciata's husband died of an illness a year before the killings started, leaving her with two sons and two daughters. A third, older daughter had recently fallen to the machete along with her husband and their two children. Aunt Anonciata's sons, her younger daughter, one of the middle daughter's sons, and a nephew lived with her. Her own sons were thirteen and twenty, the daughter was sixteen, the grandson was five, and the nephew was thirty and had a crooked leg. In a few minutes Kidende and I would be with them, our blood, our people.

We turned left on a path and entered the yard of the second house. We found our aunt in the back, cooking lunch in a pan over charcoal, the way most people in the city cooked, since they didn't have their own forests to supply firewood. Her sons and nephew were not there. Aunt Anonciata said the neighbors had stopped in a week ago and ordered her older son and the nephew to leave the house and go with them. They took them to a death ditch about ten minutes away and, with one neighbor holding the feet and another the arms, they hurled my cousins on top of the high heap of bodies in the ditch and began throwing large rocks on them, careful not to deliver an instantaneous fatal blow. Some of the rocks were the size of a soccer ball, and there were plenty of rocks on hand. Just as abicanyi throughout the country often used machetes to extend suffering through slow death by blood loss, some victims in the ditches were stoned with wicked precision that crushed but did not kill too fast. The ditch was too deep to climb out of in time to avoid being struck, but my cousins had nowhere to run anyway.

With that errand checked off the list, the neighbors visited Aunt Anonciata again. "We want your younger son too," they said, explaining that Paul Kagame, leader of the RPF, had fled Rwanda with his family at her son's age, and now Kagame was a grown man causing a lot of trouble. So they took my cousin to the ditch and threw him in. With extra-wicked precision, the rocks bombarded him in patient turn, ensuring that he would succumb more gradually than his brother and cousin had. He screamed and begged to be taken out of the pit, but his killers were only more entertained. Alone on a mountain of corpses, Kazehe – my cousin, my friend, my soccer mate – took the blows until he had no more strength to squirm, no more breath to moan. The long show was over.

Aunt Anonciata spoke with tearless grief. "Where are you boys going? We're not going to be alive much longer here." We said Standard sent us because the Interahamwe was going to kill him and that it would kill us too. She said, "I don't know where we're going to go. They're going to come for us any time now."

We ate lunch inside, with the curtains pulled. My appetite was minimal. Leaticau arrived an hour later, terrified. Being seventeen, he was a priority target and he didn't want to die in Standard's apartment. He asked Standard's friend Kamanzi to escort him to our aunt's house. That was asking the Hutu to put everything he had on the line. He could've been Baptist or Adventist or Muslim. He was a Jehovah's Witness and no ordinary one at that. He was reluctant to escort Leaticau but he agreed to do it. He told Leaticau not to look the guards in the eye when they came to the roadblock. Kamanzi showed his ID and said Leaticau was his son and that he wasn't old enough to have ID yet. The guards let them pass. Kamanzi accompanied Leaticau to Aunt Anonciata's house and then went straight home.

The rain came down hard for an hour that afternoon. When it stopped, Kamanzi sent a Hutu neighbor woman to tell us that the Interahamwes had kept their promise. They killed Hyacente and Standard around noon. She said they discovered Standard hiding in his bedroom. They didn't see Hyacente, so they went outside and looked around and finally realized he might be in the big tree behind the house. There he was. They talked him down the tree before long, probably under threat of finding somebody with a gun to shoot him, and then took him and Standard to a ditch ten minutes away. It had become filled up with bodies, so another one was dug to make just enough room for two cockroaches. The abicanyi pounded them on their heads with the ntampongano, the diabolical club designed for wrecking Tutsi heads, and tossed them in. The woman said the abicanyi were looking for us now, and that they suspected we were at our aunt's house. They just had to determine the location. Aunt Anonciata told us to leave that very moment and go to the orphanage, a four-minute walk from her house. Leaticau, Kidende and I took the path and were there in no time. The orphanage, another Hutu home, was run by Gisimba and known by his name. He was a Catholic Hutu who served God even when the world around him was falling apart. Cosmic questions such as "Where are God and the UN in all this mess?" did not stifle his outreach.

Leaticau asked to see the director. We were taken to the office, where Gisimba asked us about our situation. We told him who we were and said Aunt Anonciata had sent us to the orphanage because the abicanyi were looking for us. Gisimba said he and our aunt were practically neighbors. He knew Papa too, because the orphans went to one of the grade schools Papa directed. Gisimba knew him well.

"Do you have any news about your parents?" Gisimba asked. Leaticau told him Papa had been killed. For the first time since the genocide started, I cried. I broke down and sobbed like a kid who had just lost his father and probably his mother and probably several older siblings and had just left his little sister and brother behind and would never see them again and was tired of running away from killers. I sobbed and sobbed.

"You'll be safe here. I will shelter you," Gisimba said. "Nothing's going to happen to you. Everything's going to be okay."

My sister Polie called the apartments office to speak to Standard that day, as she had promised him when they spoke a few days earlier. The landlord's sister Bebe answered. When Bebe realized she was talking to Standard's sister, she said, "Oh, before he left, he said to tell you, 'If your younger siblings survive, please take care of them.'" She said Standard had been killed. Polie screamed, crumpled, and hung up.

The Interahamwe visited Standard's next-door neighbor Kamanzi a day or two later. He was sitting in the living room with his two-year-old daughter on his lap. They put a bullet in her head and his.

ANGER AND OATMEAL

The bunk beds in the boys' dormitory were already claimed by the regular orphans and the Tutsis who had run to hide there before Leaticau, Kidende and I arrived. A supervisor assigned us sleeping spaces on the floor and gave us adequate bedding for a good night's rest. The orphanage normally housed sixty children. We had that many people in our dormitory alone, and only about ten were children; the rest were teenagers and adults. My limited view of the compound's layout, in addition to other people's estimates, gave me the impression that Gisimba was housing two hundred people, counting the ones hiding in the ceiling. At one time it was, but the actual total climbed to more than four hundred.

Mr. Gisimba's father was Hutu. His mother was Tutsi. I was glad to be in the hands of another Hutu who cared about us. I guessed that Kidende and Leaticau felt the same, for now, but Leaticau had much more reason to fear for his existence. Violence throughout the country was often whimsical. If you didn't have ID and the abicanyi thought you were officially Tutsi, you would most likely be cut, shot or clubbed on the spot. If you had Hutu ID, the abicanyi might choose to discuss it with you and try to determine whether you were falsifying your card. Sooner or later, they would take their whimsy into the orphanage. It didn't matter that Leaticau had no ID. It wouldn't matter what he said. He was new at Gisimba, so he was a Tutsi in flight and much older than RPF leader Kagame was when he fled the country. Kidende and I were almost the same age as Kagame was back then, which made us desirable targets for the abicanyi at the orphanage, but Leaticau was an even more enticing target, because he had five years on us.

Leaticau, Kidende and I stayed together at first and gradually gravitated to other groups. Leaticau socialized with guys his age, and I hung around with former classmates of earlier grades. Since Kidende lived much farther from the capital and didn't know the other kids, he usually stuck with me.

One boy told me he had seen Papa giving money to someone. Rangira had seen Papa talking privately with Mr. Habimana at a roadblock right before the massacres in Kimisange. Cousin Safari would have told Papa about his decision to leave us with Mr. Habimana, so maybe Papa was giving the Interahamwe leader some money to cover our expenses. After his conversation with Habimana, Papa and the rest of the refugees with him went back to Kimisange and gathered with a large number of Tutsis of the Abasinga clan. The clan included Hutus, but they were not with the Tutsis. "Clan" only meant that you came from the same geographical area. My family was of the Abasingas, and Abasinga Tutsis were known for liking meat a lot. Sometimes a person would see you eating and would ask, "Are you in the Abasinga clan?" If you said yes, the person would say, "Yeah, I thought you were." It was said that Abasinga Tutsis liked meat so much they chewed the bones. As a matter of fact, the Tutsi refugees ate meat while hiding in the fields and bush, and Papa may have given money to a Tutsi family in a nearby home who invited my parents and siblings to eat with them. While they were eating at the table one morning, the abicanyi attacked. The Tutsis fled, but some of them returned later and found the food and settings on the table exactly as they had left them. Hungry as they were, they didn't touch the food, because poison was part of the abicanyi's weaponry. At any rate, if Papa gave money to the host family, they didn't have a chance to spend it.

Nobody at Gisimba talked aloud about the killings in their family. We were living together as orphans, and the assumption was that our parents had either abandoned us or were dead. Leaticau told Mr. Gisimba that Papa was dead, so that was that. And Ma Paul...I didn't know with absolute certainty what her status was, but she wasn't where Mr. Habimana said, and Aunt Cyoga hadn't seen her or heard anything about her whereabouts, so she probably had been killed, all of which meant I was a genuine orphan and I actually belonged at an orphanage except that I came from a big family and had nine older siblings and they would take care of me and tell me what to do when I didn't know what to do.

A twenty-three-year-old Tutsi man named Mupenzi tried to keep us kids mentally occupied by telling us stories and teaching us songs. We also whiled away an hour or two a day in front of the compound playing *biye* – marbles. These were an inch in diameter. Sometimes we dug a small hole in the ground and stooped a few feet from it and tried to shoot our biye in. Once yours was in, you earned the right to shoot at your opponents' *biye* that were still on the surface. To shoot, we squeezed a marble between a thumbnail and the first two fingers of the same hand and then overpowered the tension with the thumb so that the marble launched quite hard and could blast an opponent's marble away from the hole. We counted the distance between our marble and the one we hit, and gave ourselves a point for every foot of separation. The first person to fifty won the round. Leaticau's age group didn't play, and neither did we after the abicanyi became aggressive toward the orphanage.

The sound of gunfire was part of life at Gisimba. It had gotten closer as the RPF pushed the Hutu Army out of different pockets of the city. We were hearing shootouts as the takeover inched toward our part of town but not directly at us. Getting caught in the crossfire was not our worry. Our problem was the local militia – the highly territorial local Interahamwe. These men were armed with rifles, they often wore combat fatigues, and they were becoming more nervous about the RPF and angrier about all Tutsis. The disciplined RPF had proven its ability to fight against a coalition of Hutu Army and French soldiers in 1990 and 1993. France wasn't going to throw much muscle into the fight this time around. Hutu Power didn't stand a chance. Militias throughout Rwanda would have to do their work with great speed to make up for the imbalance. The killings must be merciless, must eliminate potential RPF recruits, and must be so thorough that the rebels would lose their will to fight: they would have no one to save. It was a profound miscalculation.

The abicanyi in the Gisimba neighborhood were in their twenties and thirties and were chomping at the bit to wipe us out before rebels either gave them a deadly beating or forced them and the Hutu Army out of Kigali. They were very suspicious about Mr. Gisimba. Turning kids into orphans was easy enough for killers, but obliterating or ransacking the orphanage was problematic. Some of the kids were Hutu, some were a mix, many were known Tutsis, and all were in Hutu Gisimba's care. Special permission from a political higher-up might be required for attacking the orphanage. Furthermore, Mr. Gisimba was a highly respected orphanage director and was able, for a while, to keep the abicanyi away from us by giving them money, food, or pharmaceuticals from the clinic.

Tension increased after my first two weeks at the orphanage. The militia wanted to know how many people Mr. Gisimba was sheltering and who they were. A Hutu friend of some of the older orphans came in and looked around without threatening anyone, and later began coming in to take away older residents. Gisimba sometimes pleaded successfully for the abicanyi to leave them alone, and sometimes not. Militia members who came from other areas weren't so impressed with him and didn't always listen to him or bargain with him.

Going into the dormitories allowed the Interahamwe to check on potential RPF recruits and to handpick an adult or an occasional teenager, especially of larger stature, to help meet its passion for killing cockroaches. The Interahamwe entered our dormitory more frequently as the weeks went by. At the same time, more people were seeking shelter at Gisimba every other day or so. Abicanyi who came into my dormitory found children five years old and up, teenagers, and adults up to about thirty years of age. Other Tutsi adults were hiding above the ceiling. Some were government workers, some were business people who allegedly supported the RPF. They were on the most-wanted list. Some of their names circulated in our conversation, but we never saw or heard the fugitives themselves. They didn't use our bathroom, didn't eat in our dining hall, but they were there and most of them were getting along well enough.

The orphanage had no gate. The militia showed up unannounced or knocked at the main door and somebody let them in. We preferred a knock. It became our signal to sit on the floor or lay down on our bedding to minimize our size and not stand out. When abicanyi entered, I always made sure to mingle with kids my age and younger who were the regular residents of the orphanage. Their safety seemed more certain than mine. We had no way of knowing what specifications would interest the abicanyi on a given visit. They never spoke to me while they walked around the dorm and randomly ordered an individual to stand: "Get up!" If the guy hesitated, he was hit with the butt of the gun and had no choice but to get up on his feet. Then the abicanyi would look him over and, if they saw a potential RPF recruit, they would holler profanities and "Let's go!" and lead the guy out the door. He would never be seen again.

We began asking each other, "Who did they take today?" Whoever it was, the poor guy was shot or chopped and thrown into a death ditch. One of the first people they took was the orphanage nurse. She had been there for years. Her husband was a successful businessman who allegedly supported the RPF. He was one of the most-wanted Tutsis in the area and was up in the ceiling, while the couple's two children were living down below with the rest of us. A story was circulating that the man had died after Hutus drove six-inch spikes into his skull. The abicanyi could not confirm the story with a corpse, but they were able to take his wife and, while they were at it, prevent her from treating injuries and illnesses on the compound.

They entered our dorm on another day, selected a man who looked to be almost thirty, walked him outside and fired upon him on the other side of our wall. Supervisors forbade us to watch from our windows, but it was quite enough to hear the three shots. Thirty years old. Thirty years of growing up, loving family, going to school, playing soccer with friends and classmates, drinking Watusi milk, eating potatoes cooked in butter, finding a place in the job market, drinking banana wine, starting a family, trying to get along with neighbors. The man was left where he fell. The orphanage staff had to find a way to remove and bury his body.

Leaticau's turn to be evaluated came soon enough. He was lying in a lower bunk bed. "Stand up!" a killer yelled. Leaticau stood. The Hutu looked the Tutsi up and down. He knew Leaticau wasn't a regular. "Go back and sit down!" he said. Then he selected the guy sitting in a bed next to my brother. "Stand up! Let's go!" Another victim never to be seen again.

Mupenzi, the volunteer children's activities director, was still trying to keep us distracted and busy, but the escalating danger dominated our minds. We laughed less, stayed indoors, and sat around more. We worried that we were all going to die, and we had nowhere else to go. When new kids arrived, somebody gave them a simple orientation: Don't go outside. Don't speak too loudly. If the Interahamwe come in, get down and don't look at them.

Gunfire became nonstop during the daytime. Some of the older residents talked about running away. Two of them in their twenties took off one night, and I heard in the morning that they had been caught and killed. Leaticau was talking with peers about making an evening getaway to Rebero, but the Hutu regime maintained control of Mount Kigali, which was only a few miles from the orphanage, and at hour-long intervals we watched exchanges of rocket fire and mortar explosions in the city. Rebero would be a risky two-hour walk away and would have to happen at night, when things quieted down. Leaticau didn't want me tagging along. He was afraid I couldn't run fast enough to keep up, and that I could be captured and killed. I told him I'd go with him if he left. We'd have to stay off the road and stay in the bush and paths and try to follow as straight a line as possible in order not to increase the travel distance too much. We knew our way, even if we got lost temporarily. The only reason we'd get lost would be due to avoiding usual routes because of roadblocks, houses or areas that made us too visible. But Leaticau still didn't want me to go with him.

I couldn't tell what was happening in the girls' dormitories. We never saw them, except in the hallway on their way to supper, the only meal of the day. It was served in the small dining room where we went in turns.

We were constantly hungry. Some of the regular orphans had access to more food, perhaps through connections with the cooks. These kids showed up around noon with cooked oatmeal in a three-ounce tuna can and offered to make a trade with anyone who promised half their supper in return. It was tempting. Cold and without sugar or raisins, the unsweetened oatmeal looked like grilled steak and potatoes to a stomach being gnawed by hunger that would not be satisfied even by a full ration of the six-o'clock beans and rice.

One dealer who was bigger and older than I pitched the offer to me. I gave him my word, and he gave me his oatmeal. It was delightful, not enough, but unusually good when suppertime was so far in the future. Using my thumb and two fingers, I pulled one measured clump at a time out of the little can. Nobody asked for even a nibble. They knew the deal and what I had sacrificed and what they were not willing to sacrifice, painful as it was to watch me enjoying my bland, sumptuous rolled oats all by myself. The final bite was something to lament, and I also mourned the loss of half my supper in advance.

When supper came that evening, I ate my whole ration before the dealer had a chance to get his share. He had looked forward to a supper and a half. He said he had given up his midday oatmeal and he was going to beat me up. Then he head-butted me. That was a trade I could live with – a head-butt for a three-ounce-can of cold oatmeal. But he wanted more. He ate half my supper the next day.

WINDOWS

Civilian street traffic diminished during my seven weeks at Gisimba, from May 8 to June 29, but more adults and children came in search of shelter every other day. Aunt Anonciata's sixteen-year-old daughter, Leatitia, and one of our aunt's grandsons who was Rousseau's age arrived a week after I did. Our aunt came a week later. Although abicanyi in her neighborhood had not threatened her, she lived alone and had a gut feeling that her life hung in the balance.

My dormitory had one bathroom – right next to the space on the floor that was my bed. Fifty to sixty boys going in and out of it meant that the door was constantly being opened and closed, pushing stinky air across my face. The odor came to me in full strength before thinning out in the larger living space. Besides the small windows in the bathroom, four larger ones in the wall facing the street gave us a wide view to that part of the world. The window at each end had horizontal glass panes, about thirty-six inches wide and eight inches high, that opened outwardly as you moved a lever in the middle. These windows were connected by a pair that opened vertically. All four windows formed a single unit protected on the outside with airy, crisscross bars that you could put your head through, not your whole body. The windows were usually open, but ventilation was stifled by the cloth curtains that remained closed except when we moved them just enough to have a peek at whatever was going on in front of the compound.

The air around my bedding was enough to drive an unaccustomed person to the windows. For me, however, it was the scent of survival because, when the abicanyi barged into our quarters to harass us or to choose the next person to kill, they always chose from the front and middle of the room, and my bed was the farthest from the front.

Safe as I felt there, I wanted to be outside playing marbles again with the regular orphans I knew from school. I blended in pretty well with them, but they weren't going outside anymore either. Even before Mr. Gisimba forbade everyone to play out there, Leaticau had commanded me to stay inside after he found out that one of our Hutu neighbors may have seen me. The militia was agitated and eager to destroy the orphanage and had sized up Leaticau once and let him go, but he knew they would eventually take him away. That's why he and some other guys were planning an escape. If something didn't happen soon, they'd make a run for it and I would follow Leaticau wherever he went. He couldn't stop me. I wasn't going to be left behind again by a big brother.

The need for ventilation had a lot to do with urine, and urine had a lot to do with shoes. All of us boys had shoes. It's possible that some kids arrived at the orphanage without them if killers chased them out of their homes before they had a chance to fully dress. We wore shoes at all times in the dorm to keep from losing them and because we didn't want to step barefoot on the urine that dampened the bathroom floor and was tracked all over the dorm. The bathroom had three stalls on the left side, each with a door and the typical hole in the floor. Everyone stood to pee, and not everyone was the best shot. Urine pooled in the middle of the bathroom and was distributed by constant foot traffic.

The doors on the stalls didn't click shut, but they didn't swing open either. Privacy was respected. When you went in for a bowel movement, you squatted over the hole in the floor and you didn't steady yourself by putting a hand on the wet floor. You had to keep your balance, and if you got tired of squatting, you stood up for a few moments and squatted again. Finishing as quickly as possible was a good idea, and so was planning ahead for toilet paper. We made our own. To do this, we took a sheet of paper from a school notebook and broke down its fibers in several steps. First we crumpled the paper into a ball. Then we flattened it out, held it at its ends with both hands, and rubbed the palm of one hand against the paper, pushing against the other hand in a sliding motion, starting near the wrist and moving toward the knuckles and back down toward the wrist, repeating the procedure until, in five to ten seconds, the paper was soft enough for even the choosiest human bottom, by our standards. The procedure was customary at home.

Along the right wall of the bathroom was a trough with several faucets where we washed our hands and dried them on our clothes. The dormitory itself went uncleaned, but none of us complained about our living conditions. War was being waged in the vicinity. The abicanyi could barge into our room at any time to remove and kill more of us. Our overcrowded, uncleaned quarters were the least of our worries. My roommates, however, were good about keeping the bathroom stalls tolerable.

During the weeks I had been on the run and away from home, I accumulated dirt, perspiration and lice under the waistband of the black and red athletic shorts I wore as underwear. The lice bit me and caused itching and irritation on my waist and scalp. The other boys had the same problem. We couldn't get all the lice out of our scalps, but we could pluck them off our waists. We killed one louse at a time, placing it on one thumbnail and mashing it with the other and letting the bug fall to the floor. When the lice were too abundant and annoying to handle one by one, I let them fall off my fingers to the floor. They were shortly trampled under many feet.

I remember bathing only once. We collected rainwater by putting buckets and a fifty-five-gallon drum under the gutter. It was enough for washing ourselves, but not enough for doing laundry. If my family used to take big loads of dirty clothes to the fountain, you can imagine how much water would be needed for my dormitory's laundry. The only time I washed my clothes was on a day of hard rain that kept falling and puddling on the back porch, which had a large cement slab shaped so that rain ran into the middle of it and then away from the building. I don't know who, but someone said we were going to France. People were going to come and get us and take us to the land whose language we studied in school. We would kind of live happily ever after. When I saw other kids washing their clothes to make themselves presentable to the nice French people none of us had yet seen, I started washing my clothes too. The rain gathering in the middle of the back porch was sufficient for soaking and scrubbing and rinsing our clothes as our families did at the fountains. With soap in hand, I washed my pants, my shirt and my T-shirt. I don't think I washed my black and red shorts. We hung our clothes to dry on a rope that went from one tree to another, and waited for the rescue.

In his book, *Shake Hands with the Devil*, General Roméo Dallaire, commander of the United Nations peacekeeping force in Rwanda during 1993-1994, describes a French effort to bring orphans to France for the duration of the genocide (pp. 367, 412-413). That orphanage was not far from Gisimba, and the effort – which was badly bungled – probably generated the rumor that excited us kids at Gisimba. When the French did not come and get us, we fell into a state of prolonged disappointment. Our days were boring, our bellies hungry. The restless abicanyi told the orphanage director they were going to kill him and blow up the whole compound with their rocket-propelled grenades. Gisimba Damas fled to Saint Michel Catholic Church and left his brother, Jean-Francois, in charge.

I hadn't seen Gisimba Damas since my first day at the orphanage. He was always busy trying to pacify the abicanyi while handling his administrative burden. He had no time to spend with us children, so he assigned older regular orphans – eighteen to twenty years old – to supervise us and keep us in good cheer, as far as possible. Some of them were Hutus, some were Tutsis, and they were kind to all of us.

The Tutsi rebels had methodically worked their way deeper into Kigali, which had a population of about two hundred thirty-five thousand. Some of the rebels were moving in our general direction, and Leaticau and some other guys his age were unwilling to risk an escape that would put them in the crossfire of battle. A noose was tightening around the government's army and the local militias. At the same time, international powers were finally putting a noose of their own on the Hutu government, which in turn was telling its genocidal wings, including the militia that was threatening to blow us up at any moment, to show restraint in killing. The massacres must continue, swiftly and thoroughly, but they must be done when international eyes were not looking. Any Rwandan government needed foreign support in order to survive. There was no point in wiping out the Tutsis and moderate Hutus if the majority party lost favor with the rest of the world. Rwanda would descend into hopeless disarray. Hutu majority leaders wouldn't be able to secure their objectives. The world had turned a blind eye for a while, but the extremists' brutality was now so well documented and sickening that nations couldn't dance around reality anymore with silly verbiage about definitions and unconfirmed claims. Even France, long-time friend of the Hutu majority, had begun to resist the genocide with stern disapproval and by offering some protection to some victims in some places.

But that didn't mean the local Interahamwe wasn't going to blow us up. Nobody besides the RPF and a pocket of Tutsi victims here and there was actually fighting the extremists. On June 28, the militia surrounded the orphanage and was ready to kill us and destroy the orphanage, when they were surprised by the appearance of a Muzungu named Carl Wilkens, the only American who had stayed in Rwanda. He was country director of ADRA, the humanitarian arm of the Seventh-day Adventist Church, and he had come with water. If Wilkens were black, the militia might not have paid any attention to him. But he was obviously a foreigner and he was talking on his radio.

I moved the curtain on the front window just enough to see the Muzungu in a light-blue vest that read "ADRA." He was standing by our water tank and filling it from a container in the bed of a small truck. What I couldn't see were the dozens of Interahamwe who had taken positions to bring down our entire compound. In a 2011 article of *The Guardian*, Gisimba Jean-Francois says the militia's boss told his men in Kinyarwanda not to do anything while the Muzungu was there. Wilkens, who does not speak Kinyarwanda, details much of the June 28 standoff in his book, *I'm Not Leaving*. While Jean-Francois was begging the foreigner not to leave, Wilkens excused himself and went to seek help from the ruthless Colonel Tharcisse Renzaho, mayor of Kigali. The colonel wasn't at his office, but the recently appointed and equally ruthless Prime Minister Kambanda happened to be there. He responded to Wilkens' pleading to protect the orphanage by instructing another official to prevent violence against it.

In his book, Wilkens notes that Kambanda told him, "We are aware of the situation." We orphans had been told a few weeks earlier that Gisimba Damas had fled to Saint Michel Catholic Church to save his neck and to prepare to relocate everyone who was at the orphanage. He called Kambanda, whom he knew, and told him the militia was going to kill his orphans. That would explain why Kambanda told Wilkens that he knew of the threat. Wilkens' actions saved hundreds of lives by making the issue a priority, reinforced by the presence of a foreign witness. The local militia's boss must have decided to delay the attack when Wilkens and his radio left the orphanage, perhaps thinking that Wilkens had gone to discuss it with somebody who mattered to the Hutu government. According to *The Guardian*, an army major came to our compound with a dozen soldiers and told them to shoot anyone who attacked us. He told Jean-Francois that the soldiers would move all the residents and staff the next day.

The next day was June 29. Hutu soldiers arrived before noon with six buses and entered the compound. They told us to get out of our dormitory. "Move, move, move!" they shouted. "Don't take anything!" Within twenty minutes, the girls and boys of Gisimba Orphanage boarded the buses and packed in until there wasn't room for another person to stand. The soldiers didn't tell us where we were going, and they were not finished with trying to kill some of us. We felt that our prospects could be good or bad. We all remained quiet.

The people in the attic came out into the light too, including the influential businessman who was the husband of the nurse who had been taken away, and another man who was president of a political party that allegedly helped finance the RPF. The Hutu soldiers were stunned when they saw the two men. They had stopped looking for the nurse's husband because they'd heard he had been captured and killed. Now it was obvious that he had outfoxed them, but at least they had killed his wife. One soldier cursed and slammed his rifle on the ground. They wanted to kill the two men and their families on the spot, but they were under orders to harm no one.

The buses pulled away from the orphanage toward an unstated destination. We didn't pass any roadblocks, but we did see fresh corpses on the side of the road. A dog was standing on one of them. Several miles down the road, we found ourselves at Saint Michel Catholic Church. Without speaking to us, the soldiers dropped us off at the main entrance. The facility was larger than the orphanage building and had a basement sectioned into rooms with electric lights. One side of the basement was open to a campus much larger than the Gisimba property.

The buses and soldiers left. A half hour later, I was standing outside with Leaticau and Kidende when Aunt Anonciata came up to us and said, "They're taking us to the high school. They're saying the older people have to go to the high school because it's too crowded here." The Interahamwe started loading adults into a pickup truck a few feet from me. The crowd was blocking the driveway to the road, and the loading process was chaotic but calm. Aunt Anonciata said she would be going with the second load. Then someone warned the adults to get off the truck because they'd be murdered at the high school. It was happening to people in other places. The Interahamwe left empty-handed.

In a bizarre deal involving reasonable cash, Carl Wilkens arranged for the Interahamwe to transport pots and pans and blankets and personal effects from the orphanage to the church. We were five or ten minutes from the large Hutu army base, Camp Kigali; the same distance in the other direction from the genocidal national radio station, which had been forced to broadcast from another location; and three minutes from the infamous Hôtel de Mille Collines. We didn't have enough blankets to go around, and for three nights some of us slept on the church's courtyard, shivering under the stars. Then we were moved indoors. It finally did look like everything was going to be okay, although I didn't like being only twenty-five yards from the road that went to Camp Kigali, the hotel and the national radio station. However, I didn't see a need to go to France anymore. I felt safer than I had felt in a long time.

The night of July 3 was noisy. A loud and long convoy of big trucks and other military vehicles passed by the church. The Hutu army was running for its own life now, slipping through the noose. The convoy fired not a shot, not a cannon, not a rocket. The next day – July 4 – the RPF declared the city under rebel control. Some of RPF soldiers visited Saint Michel. For me and everybody else who had sheltered at the orphanage, the genocide was over. Fighting would continue elsewhere for a few more weeks, but for us it was over. We were free. By July 7, my brother and cousin and I had gone to live with Aunt Anonciata at her house, and this time the abicanyi would not bother us. They had fled, died or gone into hiding after turning us into orphans. Soon many of them would be orphans themselves, or widows, widowers, childless, alone, penniless. We would grieve similar losses, but never would any of them express the least bit of regret for slaughtering my family and our hearts.

BONES

Even today some Rwandan survivors have not buried their loved ones. We Kagabos didn't bury ours until July 1996. And even then we didn't bury them all; we never found Ingabire. The country was disoriented and dizzy after one hundred days of genocide. Bodies were everywhere and they were mixed up, often unrecognizable or unrecoverable. Some bodies were lost or totally destroyed. You have to be mentally, physically and financially ready to do burials that follow massive brutality. It's not an easy task. It is, for a while, an inconceivable one. It surely is not normal. Those of us Kagabos who were still in Rwanda had moved to Aunt Josephine's home and were too young to manage a burial. It wasn't on our priority list, nor on Aunt Josephine's. The main reason for delaying a burial, however, was the fear that some abicanyi were still around, laying low, especially in rural areas like our town of Kimisange.

Two years after the slaughters ended, the time was right, our family was ready. Damas took the lead as the oldest sibling, accompanied by the next oldest, Pigeon (Jean-Marie), since Standard was no longer available. To bury our deceased family members, we had to know where they were, and much of that information would have to come from our neighbors, the families of the killers. Our Tutsi friends had moved out of the neighborhood, the ones who hadn't been killed. Their lives were still at risk, their houses were destroyed, and the memory of abicanyi was still fresh in their minds. Remnants of the Interahamwe hung around, desiring to kill more cockroaches despite the RPF's overwhelming victory. Some people adopted the bloodthirsty attitude of their relatives in the Interahamwe. I saw Rangira's former classmate Rugema at Saint Michel Church the day the RPF captured Kigali. He was so happy to have survived and was ready to move on with the challenge of life without his parents. He was determined. He was smiling. He trusted that the Hutu-Tutsi conflict was behind him. He looked forward to resuming friendships with Hutus in our area. He was fatally poisoned soon after. The news of Rugema's death devastated me and put me on guard every time I went back home.

Damas and Pigeon approached our neighbors for help in locating our deceased family. Many of them didn't want to disclose the facts, for fear of being jailed. Others were cooperative and reliable sources. They revealed where their relatives and other abicanyi had killed and dumped our loved ones. Dada's friend Fifi was no longer in our neighborhood but she provided the whereabouts of Jolie's and Dada's remains. With this precise information, it took Damas and Pigeon only one day to gather the bones and the deteriorated clothing on them. The job was all the easier because the bodies – the pieces of them – were in shallow graves and covered with superficial mounds of dirt. The corpses of about a million Tutsis and moderate Hutus had littered the Rwandan soil and waterways in 1994, and people who lived by the remains had to do something to get the corpses out of their sight, out of their nostrils, out of their way. Blankets of soil were a quick way to mask the horrors and the stench of devastation.

Damas and Pigeon bought two wooden caskets and took them to the Kagabo farm. Damas asked the Hutu caretaker of our property to find field workers he could pay to dig the graves in the backyard of our former home. When the digging was done, the bones lay distributed in the caskets, three skulls in one, four in the other. Papa's remains came with his mostly shredded clothes. The office keys in one of his pants pockets were left there. After a Catholic funeral the next day, with many relatives and friends in attendance, the caskets were lowered into the ground and covered with the backfill. Our Hutu neighbors did not attend. It was unthinkable in everyone's mind. Polie was absent also, as she was out of the country and pregnant with her first child.

Papa had bought additional land from neighbors as our family grew. His intention was to be able to give a hectare (two and half acres) to his children when they came of age and married. Papa always took Ingabire to see a new plot so that one of us would know what we owned in case anything happened to Papa. Tutsi men and women who were persecuted by the Hutu majority government in 1959 and the following decade assumed they might very well be run off their property or killed. Around 1990, many Tutsi men who were educated or had good jobs were imprisoned for months and tortured. My godfather and other friends of Papa were too. On my way home from school, I used to pass a pub owned by a Tutsi man and frequented by Tutsi men from that neighborhood who shared a drink after a day's work. I am sure they discussed the dangers their families faced. Each had at least five children, and all these families perished during the genocide, confirming their firm assumptions that their freedoms and lives hung by a thread. Like these men, my parents were plagued by the wicked extremes that could befall the offspring they brought into the world without our consent.

I worried for the longest time that Papa would be arrested, but he never was. Once I was with a little boy, the youngest of his family, who burst into tears when he heard that his godfather (and mine), Jean-Léonard, was released from prison. He ran to Jean-Léonard's house to be with him again. The boy's dad was the godfather of one of my brothers, and Papa was the godfather of that boy's older brother. Then came the genocide. The abicanyi murdered the boy along with his father, his mother, two sisters and a brother. They killed the whole wonderful family, just as they killed much of ours, just as Papa feared while planning for the future and buying land.

Now that Ingabire isn't here either, Polie speculates that we have more hectares than we know of. Some of our plots were a long distance from our home. That doesn't mean another family hasn't taken them for their own during all these years. Life does go on and people need land to make a living back home. Many houses and hectares switched hands after the genocide, when more than a million people fled or returned.

My twin sisters – Polie and Jolie – were six when Ingabire was born. The first three siblings were boys, about two years apart. After the long break following the twins' birth, their mother's pregnancy with Ingabire went well, but she died of blood loss a day and a half after delivering him. Polie, a nurse, still laments that Ingabire wasn't able to benefit from the intimacy and nutrition of breast-feeding, but the powdered infant formula he gulped down didn't keep him from growing tall, strong and sociable. The last favor Polie asked of him was to get her new suitcase from a friend's house where she left it after buying it at a Kigali supermarket. She was twenty-three, dressed up, and unwilling to be seen walking all the way home with an extra-large suitcase on top of her head. Ingabire proudly helped his sister by bringing it home on his head. Then our family accompanied her in a large taxi van to the airport, where she boarded a plane to Switzerland.

Ingabire was stabbed to death during a skirmish with the Hutu Army while participating in a rescue operation. When a loved one goes unfound, your mind plays tricks on you. The loss is never quite resolved. You theorize about the missing person's location and condition. Polie theorizes that Ingabire could be wandering in the bush, out of his mind, or maybe in the hands of extremists who torture him. Rangira manufactures these possibilities and suggests them in a form of dark humor that has a place among survivors. He says Ingabire is out there somewhere. His suggestions get stuck in Polie's head and make her wonder if they might be true, all the while knowing they cannot be, although she cannot prove that they aren't, and so they could be, though she is certain they are not.

They are not. I have accepted Ingabire's death.

Citizens throughout Rwanda looked for their deceased loved ones for years after the genocide. During the 2000s, the government invited survivors to take the remains to memorial centers that had been erected in various areas of the country. That sounded like a great idea to Polie, who had missed the first burial of our family members. She wanted to dig them up and inter them at the big Kigali Genocide Memorial Centre in Gisozi. Polie prepared herself deeply so that she would be able to execute her plan – a well guarded secret – in 2007 when all of us surviving Kagabos were in Rwanda for a reunion and the second burial. We rented one side of a duplex and spent three weeks together. On one side of the house was an outdoor faucet that only Polie was thinking about.

On a typical day of the faraway past, getting to the gravesites we were going to dig up could have been accomplished by going through the front door of our main house and out the back door, taking ten or fifteen steps and then going into the secondary house, the smaller one that Mr. Saint Habimana and his crew were remodeling inside and out when the killings started, then past the outdoor kitchen area and a fence, and that's where the graves were. We buried Mama Volks there years earlier.

But our main house had long been picked apart and destroyed, and the earth-and-wood walls had dissolved into uneven, lumpy ground. The secondary house was still standing with its doors and windows removed. The yard was rough. My older sisters and an aunt their age who had lived with us for a while used to sweep the yard around the main house with homemade brooms, short-handled ones of stout bristles made with a specific grass bundled at the base of the handle. The three girls swept the front yard every Saturday and made our place look beautiful. The mostly organic debris was swept into round containers and carried on the girls' heads to a deep, twelve-foot-square pit behind the outhouse. The pit was one big casserole of garbage, dirty banana leaves from the cowshed, and cow manure, all in a constant state of decomposition that produced fertilizer. One Tutsi hid in a banana-beer pit during the genocide, but he would not have done well in a compost pit.

We asked Hutu neighbors to help dig up the remains, and because they felt ashamed, they gladly volunteered for the rugged work of removing five or six feet of dirt from both graves. They or their people had killed our loved ones, and it was fitting that they help dig them up so we could move them again. Neighbors took turns busting the sod with hoes and shoveling it out, throwing it past the edges to leave room for standing around the hole. July is dry in that part of Rwanda, so the soil was easier to work.

The father of Rurangwa – the school principal who wanted to date Jolie – came too. Polie wanted to tell the father, "I heard Rurangwa helped kill Jolie," but she didn't say it. He said his son must have regretted his involvement in the killings. He said Rurangwa had joined the Interahamwe and that God punished him for it, letting him die like an animal in the forest, without mourners or a burial. He had run to the Congo and probably died a wretched death from cholera.

A former elementary schoolmate of Jolie who had driven Polie in an SUV to the Kagabo home became angry when he saw our Hutu neighbors digging up our family. "Let's do it ourselves," he said to

Polie. But we were more than happy to let the neighbors proceed. The whole process lasted from ten in the morning until midafternoon.

Bones came into view before wood. The coffins had completely dissolved after more than a decade in the soil. Except for backfilling the holes later, the rest of the work was for Tutsis, so the neighbors went home. There was no shaking of hands, no warm goodbyes, just a little bit of solemn appreciation. We understood each other, we understood the moment. The Tutsis now took turns climbing into the double grave one at a time, scraping out the bones and clothing with their hands. They placed the artefacts on a thin canvas spread out on the ground above, until all the pieces of seven disconnected skeletons had been extracted. We tied the corners of the canvas the way we used to tie a sheet to haul laundry to the fountain and back, and put the precious collection in the back of the SUV.

Then Polie revealed a secret: she was going to wash the bones.

Damas said no. He said she'd be overtaken by unbearable grief. He said, no, no, no. Polie said, "You can't stop me." We drove to the rented house, set the bag of bones by the outside faucet, and had a late lunch.

Soon Polie was setting out half a dozen laundry tubs. She set rented chairs around a rented coffee table for anyone who wanted to sit and observe. This furniture would seat guests the next day during a traditional gathering. Under normal circumstances, a burial is followed by an invitation to "wash our hands," a reference to washing the dirt off your hands after burying someone. You're really just getting together with family and friends over refreshments and talking about the deceased.

At first, we stood at a distance from Polie and the bones. We didn't want to touch them or be anywhere near them. She filled two tubs with water for pre-rinsing, two with soapy water, and two more with water for final rinsing. Our deceased were all jumbled up on the canvas that Polie untied and opened, a display that seemed better than being in the lonely, shallow graves they were in before Damas and Pigeon found them. Papa was found alone, with his head off. Ma Paul had been dumped into an outdoor toilet. Jolie was beheaded and was with an old lady none of us knew. Out of respect for her, my brothers collected her bones too. Dada was alone and beheaded. Standard and Cousin Hyacente were found in the small ditch dug just for them. And now everyone was in a big happy pile and ready for an afternoon bath.

Polie put on a pair of latex gloves and lifted Papa's head. She was certain it was him. The teeth in the skull were identical to hers. She held him for a long time, ten minutes, and gazed into the face of the man who was everything to her. How she adored him! She put Papa in a tub of clear water and wiped the loose dirt off him. Next, she gave him a deeper cleaning in the soapy water, then rinsed him in another tub. She didn't want to let go of him. The more I watched my sister love our father's remains, the bolder I became to touch him myself...later.

I saw Papa's key chain lying by the house while Polie carried on. At least ten keys, and some must have been for his offices and classrooms. They were rusty and packed with dirt, but intact. They reminded me of what he used to tell us — that we were working for our own sakes, not his, and that one day he would not be around to benefit from the fruits of our success. I became angry in that moment and wondered what I should do with the keys — keep them or leave them. I left them in the backyard grass by Polie. I left them to be forgotten. Nobody ever said a word about them. I wish I had kept them. I wish I could hold them in my hands, a piece of Papa, hold them with hands that have nothing else of him to hold.

Maman Paul was my mother, not Polie's, but she had been very good to our dad's first six children, raising them as her own, and they loved her. Polie held Ma Paul briefly and then washed her. Surprisingly, Polie wasn't crying. She had prepared herself, and she also did not want Damas to halt the process in order to protect her. As she went on washing, everyone but Damas warmed up to the process and became interested by Polie's commentaries. We helped dry. Polie did not speak to the bones. She mused aloud: "Who is this one?" "Is this Jolie?" "It does look like it's probably her." I started wondering too.

Stella and Rousseau were not among the bones. They had been rescued by the RPF two or three nights after Kidende and I left them behind at Aunt Cyoga's home. It was another of the amazing rescues the rebels pulled off in hostile territory. If it happened three nights after Kidende and I left Aunt Cyoga's house, then it was Stella's birthday present. She turned ten on May 4, the same day Polie called from Geneva, Switzerland and spoke with Standard. He told her he heard that Papa and Jolie had been killed. He didn't tell me.

Stella describes the rescue:

> After the RPF took us to Byumba where they had taken over, things were good. But before we got there, we went to 3 other places, and we would spend 1, 2 or 3 nights there.

> When we left our aunt's house where Kaka left us, we went to Rebero, an RPF camp. The first time I saw dead bodies was on our way there. It was at night, of course, and there were many of us being rescued, so we would walk in single file with one RPF soldier in the front and one in the back. We saw dead bodies here and there on the road.

> We spent maybe 3 days at Rebero, but we were still in danger. Rockets were fired at us. We were not allowed to wander outside or cook during the day, because the Hutus would see smoke and start firing rockets!

> So we had to go to another place called Nyanza. We went at night. Extremists had killed a lot of Tutsis in Nyanza a few days before and stacked up their bodies. We had to walk through them and at times had to step on them to get to where we were going.

> We spent one day there, and then had to move again. We went to Remera and stayed in some rich guy's building for one night. Then we went to Byumba where we stayed for about 2 months! We were traveling by foot to those places, except when we went to Byumba there was a truck that took us.

It was wonderful to meet up with my sister and brother a month after the genocide ended and to find them alive and well. Three aunts cared for us – Cyoga, Anonciata and Josephine. Only recently did I learn we aren't related to Cyoga by blood. We gave her the title "Aunt" after the genocide because of her role in our survival. Rousseau and Stella returned to stay with Aunt Cyoga until sometime in August. Then they came to live with Papa's sister, Josephine, who had taken me in. Rangira and Leaticau joined us and Aunt

Josephine's five children. Counting her husband, we became a household of twelve.

With the landlord's permission, we put the bones on sheets to dry in the front room of the other side of the duplex. We held the skulls lovingly and discussed them.

"This has to be Standard."

"What makes you think so?"

"His slender face."

"Look, this is Jolie."

"Oh, no, this is."

"You think so?"

"I think it might be Hyacente."

I took time to hold every single head. I tried to imagine who they were and how they looked when they were alive. I wasn't certain that Polie was right about which head was Papa's, but her commentary made the ordeal less spooky and more familial. I went through the heads more than once to identify and contemplate them. I felt some anger. I wondered, *How in the world did they get this way? They should be standing here talking with me!*

Ma Paul's head. It seemed like hers as I rotated it slowly, lovingly, yearningly. My mother was killed at age forty-nine. She enjoyed spending one-on-one time with me when she had a chance, which isn't easy in a big family. She would ask me to go with her to help pick vegetables and fruits from the fields, or to help her sort tiny pebbles from dried red beans that had been beaten out of their pods with a big stick. She told me stories from her past while we worked. She said she was almost killed by lightning while walking home in a rainstorm when she was a girl. She sat under a tree that shielded her from the rain. When the rain slowed, she started walking again. A few seconds later, a lightning bolt hit the tree and knocked it to the ground. I wouldn't be here to enjoy life if she had stayed under that tree.

She used to get sick in her stomach from worms in the drinking water. She woke us kids up one night and gathered us in the living room to pray with her. She was in awful misery. Holding a Bible, she told us she didn't know what she wanted to read in it, but she was going to open it and read from the page her eyes fell on. It was a unique moment, it was according to her faith, not a pattern she lived by. She read the page to us, and when she finished, we said our normal bedtime prayers and we all went back to bed.

That night I was very worried that I would lose the great woman who was my mother. She gradually recovered without having to be hospitalized and relieved of her motherly duties. I couldn't imagine not having her in my life, and now I was holding her in my hands. The son of our next-door neighbor Mr. Nyamurwano killed her. Ma Paul had run away from a massacre in Kimisange and found mercy with a Hutu friend who lived ten minutes from our house. The woman hid my mom in an outbuilding the size of a bedroom, used for keeping cows at night. The walls were solid and impossible to see through. So how did Mr. Nyamurwano's son find Ma Paul? And why did he go looking for her? It's possible that he searched the premises to see if any Kagabos were hiding there, since not all of us on the killing list had been accounted for. Or maybe the homeowner or her daughter reported my mother to the killer out of fear or revenge. The RPF had recently entered a Hutu home, probably confusing it with another home, which apparently instigated an attack inside the house to which the soldiers reacted by killing the family. That's the incident I heard Mrs. Habimana telling her husband about while I was at their house. A deadly attack by Tutsis was new to Hutus in our town. The disturbance could have motivated neighbors to report or look for hidden Tutsis.

In any case, our next-door neighbor's son apparently cornered Ma Paul in the outbuilding and beat her with the ntamponango, beat her like he was beating red beans out of their pods. Then someone lifted the wooden floor of the outside toilet and dropped her into the sewage. She was there for two years. Violet, the homeowner's daughter, told Damas and Pigeon where Ma Paul was. And now I was holding my dear mother, washed up and looking as good as a skull can look after two years in the toilet. I stared and contemplated. *Polie thinks this is her. I'm pretty sure this is her too.* At the very least, we all knew who the whole collection of bones belonged to, even if we weren't completely sure which pieces belonged to whom.

Papa's head. It did seem like him, but I had never seen him stripped down this far. Whenever he came home from work in the evening, he went to our study room to say hello and check on us. If we had finished our studies or didn't need help, we had to keep reading and studying until dinner was ready. Sometimes we got so sleepy some of us put our heads down on the study table and dozed off while one of us kept an ear out and alerted the others if Papa was coming. We'd sit up and cast a studious eye at our books. I'm sure our drowsy eyes told the truth. The only way to stay awake was to leave the room and walk around or wash our faces with cold water. Papa would repeat his goal: "Everything you are doing you are doing for your own sakes, not for mine, because one of these days I will not be around and you will be taking care of yourselves." He died at fifty-seven.

I had a silly thought when I was seven. I wondered which parent I could do without if one were to die. I couldn't answer my question. I loved them both too much to do without either one. Then I lost them both, at about the same time, which gave me a dreadful advantage – I was forced to mourn their deaths together, find out who was going to take care of me, and get on with the rest of my life.

Some of my family visited Daniel at his home in 2009, two years after the cleaning of the bones, fifteen years after the genocide. In 1994, he likely fled to the Congo ahead of the RPF's arrival in our neighborhood, and then returned from a cholera-stricken refugee camp to take his chances with justice after the new government invited all Rwandans back to the country to make a new start. All or most Tutsis had been wiped out in most neighborhoods, which offered the possibility that no victims remained to point an accusing finger. Even so, facing accusers and being put behind bars sounded better than catching cholera and becoming another of its agonizing casualties.

It was not a happy day for Daniel and his wife when Pigeon, Polie and Stella showed up in their yard. They must have felt like monsters. They must have felt...guilty. Our property was only a few hundred yards from theirs, separated by a field. Our main house had stood ruined and empty for years now, and Tutsi neighbors were long gone. Daniel's wife hurried into their house. Daniel invited the visitors in, but Polie said they would rather talk outside. Pigeon asked who killed our father and how it happened. Daniel said somebody had yelled and Papa went running out of the bush and other men killed him. It was a nonsensical answer. Nothing Daniel said shed light on Papa's death, except to convince us that Daniel was trying hard to cover his part in it.

Standard's head. It had a crevice across the top, most likely from the ntamponango. In one of Polie's phone conversations with Standard, this one on May 6, he told her "Polie, pray for us, because they're going to kill us. They just killed Kigingi." Kigingi was the fifteen-year-old son of Stella's godfather. I used my imagination to put skin and clothes back on Standard. The head was a good starting point, because it appeared to be his. Losing my father would have been easier if Standard had survived. But Standard faced the same persecution my parents did. In 1993 he worked as a veterinarian in the province of Gisenyi, on the Rwanda-Congo border, and he feared that Hutus would kill him. Things had turned pretty bad for Tutsis there and in certain other parts of the country. So he moved back to Kigali to live and work near home. Like Jolie, he was probably going to get married in a couple of years. Since he was still single and living near home again, I got to spend more time with him, and he used that time to cross-examine my academic habits and performance. He was tough on me, and he was good to me. Once in a while he invited me for lunch at his apartment on school days. I think he felt bad that I was making the forty-five-minute walk home for lunch and forty-five back. His invitations made me happy. He lived less than twenty minutes from my school, so eating lunch at his place saved me fifty minutes on the round trip.

What made Standard special as an older brother was that, although I never asked him for anything, he always knew what I liked and what made me happy. He took me to a professional soccer game and then to a classy restaurant where I had my first brochette, or kabob. He liked the restaurant because he liked the cook's brochettes. He also liked repeating the cook's name, Kafunga, emphasizing the pronunciation because it wasn't a typical Rwandan name.

As we went down a steep path that evening in early darkness, Standard told me to quit walking with both hands in my pockets. He said I could trip and fall and be seriously injured. I worked on that habit under his watchful eye.

Standard's landlord Karegeya was another of the abicanyi who fled to a refugee camp in the Congo and then returned. The Nyamirambo police arrested him and held him in jail until a local court sentenced him to prison.

Jolie's head. Another one with a big crevice in it. I couldn't tell for sure whether it was her. Jolie was the oldest sibling at home when the genocide started. Dada's friend Fifi watched from a hidden spot as Jolie and another woman were murdered in a field behind a Tutsi home where a number of people had been hiding. When the abicanyi approached the property, the Tutsis ran into the field but didn't get far. Fifi said Jolie was so hungry and exhausted that she didn't even scream while the abicanyi beat and chopped her.

Dada's head. I couldn't distinguish between all these skulls. I could dress any of them up with skin and clothing in my mind and make them whomever I wanted them to be as I thought about them and how much I loved them and would always miss them. Fifi was the last person to see Dada. That was the night Dada wanted to stop and rest and get a drink of water and Fifi warned her not to knock on the Hutu's door and Dada said she couldn't go any farther without water. So she knocked. If this was her head I was holding, it was severed with a machete by the man who opened the door and welcomed Dada in. Did that family give her a drink of water before the blade started swinging?

Hyacente's head. He lost his parents and they lost him. So many cousins and other relatives stayed at our house at different times in our family history. They kept our house full, even when some of my siblings moved out. It's good for cousins to grow up together.

The old lady's head: Whichever head was hers, I couldn't put skin on it and remember anything about her. We didn't know the woman. But we cleaned her up and loved her, held her in our hands and looked into her eyes. We treated her with the same eerie tenderness we lavished on the others. Her family, if they survived, have wondered where she is. I can only say that she was given full respects and a proper place among the fallen at the Gisozi Genocide Memorial Centre, where people from all around the globe recognize her and the others as human beings worthy of remembrance. She will not be forgotten. The many Hutus – though a very small fraction of the Hutu population – who were killed for opposing the genocide and showing sympathy to Tutsis are remembered along with this woman whose bones were collected along with Jolie's.

The Tutsi landlord called and said we had to move the bones out of that side of the duplex because some people were coming in the morning to rent it. They never came, but we moved the bones. She probably wanted us to offer her money for the space, but we didn't want to. We moved our loved ones so much that day they were probably glad when sunset came. It comes at the same time every day of the year. Six o'clock.

We brought two caskets to the house in a rented truck, put the bones in them and rearranged the living room furniture to make room for the caskets, which we closed. Relatives and friends dropped in to be with us. Rwandans have a custom of spending much more time together when someone dies, but we told our guests we were tired from a long, emotional day and that we would open the house for just one short evening. Tomorrow would be a long day with a funeral service at the church and the burials in Gisozi.

Only a few people sat inside that evening. The situation was woefully familiar to everyone who came, and we all wanted to talk about something besides those coffins and the stuff inside them. In the morning, Pigeon carefully arranged the bones in the two caskets, distributed the heads, and closed the caskets again. We had the service and the burials, and we have always wished we could have done the same for Ingabire. But our children, grandkids and great-grandkids will know where their relatives were laid to rest, and they can visit them in the underground mausoleum.

Polie says, "They were just thrown away at first. I wanted them to be peacefully laid down. We did that, and I know where they are. I'm glad they're at the memorial, because who knows how long we will own our family property?"

We couldn't bear the thought of another family buying our land and owning the graves of our loved ones. I don't know about that one old lady, but our people are right where we want them and she's welcome to stay with them for as long as she wants. "I like that they are all together," says Polie. "They're not lonely."

EPILOGUE

Forgiveness Under the Right Conditions

Kaka and Max

We believe that victims of any serious offense are rarely responsible for forgiving the people who hurt them. Some victims say they've had to forgive their assailants in order to move on with life, and then they go on to say that everyone else needs to do that for their own good. Their experience is their prescription for everyone else's healing. But most of the genocide victims we know are not struggling to forgive. They have their hands full with managing daily life and moving forward with a clear mind. All of that is easier to do when they determine not to spend their time wishing for revenge.

Max: Kaka, you said you had a plan for keeping focused every day. Tell the reader what you told me.

Kaka: I get up in the morning and ask God to give me the strength to be good to everyone I come across that day.

Max: In other words, you ask for strength to do the opposite of the evil you went through. But do you spend time wishing you could take revenge on the people who slaughtered your loved ones?

Kaka: No, I do not spend my time thinking about how I would like to hurt those cruel people. I probably would like to hurt them, but I do not let myself think on that.

Max: Do you despise them?

Kaka: Yes.

Max: Several people have told me that what you're doing is a type of forgiveness. I heard a wise priest call it one level of forgiveness. You decide not to dwell on the evil that happened. You ask God to train you to think about doing good. You don't dwell on revenge. So, I have a question: Have you forgiven your family's killers?

Kaka: How do I know whether I have forgiven them? They never came to me or to anyone in my family and apologized for what they did. None of them or their families have asked me to forgive them.

Max: And yet some people, including me, believe that you are showing some level of forgiveness.

Kaka: Okay, I get that. But most readers probably think of forgiveness as more than that, and I don't want anyone to think that I forgave my family's killers. I choose to forget about the killers so that I don't keep the anger inside of me. And being friends with other Hutus does not mean that I have reconciled with the killers. People use the word "reconciliation" incorrectly. Reconciliation should happen between two individuals who put their animosity aside and agree to coexist and work together on a regular basis. Reconciliation becomes more understandable in a one-to-one context.

Max: You and I have heard survivors say they've forgiven when they're really just trying to shut the horrible memories out of their mind. Healing a deep wound is not a solo job. It usually requires repentance and sorrow on the part of the perpetrator. Putting the responsibility to forgive on the victim is a mistake.

Kaka: I totally agree. I keep saying we have to better say what we mean so that we don't mislead people about our feelings. The genocide impacted us heavily, but most of us did not prevail by forgiving our enemies. The word "forgive" has to be used correctly. People use the word "forgive" because it sounds like a good thing to do. In almost all cases, the killer holds the key to forgiveness by admitting wrongdoing and asking to be forgiven.

Max: A widespread error is that the Bible teaches us to forgive everyone no matter what. Preachers quote Jesus on the cross – "Father, forgive them, because they don't know what they're doing."

But Jesus consistently taught that sins would be forgiven under certain conditions. He said, "Unless you repent, you too will die in your sins." Lots of Scripture passages are misinterpreted by people who want to teach that forgiveness is the victim's responsibility. Forgiveness is made possible under certain conditions.

You don't tell rapists, "Well, we believe in God and we're taught to forgive and forget. So, forget about our accusations. Forget about justice. We'll talk to your victims and instruct them to forgive you so they can experience freedom." No. We process the offenders, and forgiveness might happen later, under the right circumstances.

We don't have to approach this as just a religious issue, but consider the Lord's Prayer: "Forgive us...as we forgive...." Even Jesus taught that we are to forgive people who ask to be pardoned. However, he went for the heart, for a change of heart and behavior. If we forgive repentant people, God will forgive us when we repent. The burden is not on the offended.

Kaka: Well said, Max. Many of the 1994 genocide survivors have moved away from their hometowns in order to move on and rebuild their lives, and to avoid being tormented by constant anger and reminders of horrible experiences and possible encounters with perpetrators that are back from serving their time in prison. The rebuilding process is very difficult for many survivors. Many are orphans, widows and widowers. Many aren't able to move away. They don't have any choice but to stay and use some of the resources that were left when they returned from their rescue havens.

And the perpetrators will probably never have a chance to approach the survivors who are no longer in their hometowns. They won't have the chance to ask for forgiveness, even if they desired to do so. But that doesn't matter to survivors who have in many cases struggled to survive after the genocide and who rarely if ever go back home. They haven't forgiven, but relocating has made it easier to forget in order to move on with their lives.

Max: Take marriage problems. There are millions of cases of spouses in conflict, where one partner is ready to forgive but it has absolutely no impact on the chance for reconciliation, because the other partner is neither interested nor repentant. So, forgiveness is sometimes irrelevant and certainly ineffective, because one person isn't participating.

It's a big mistake to tell victims that they can heal only if they forgive. Forgiveness, simply put, is not always an issue.

Take the guy who shot up the people at the local Noblesville, Indiana school. Would we tell the mother of the thirteen-year-old girl that she has to forgive the shooter? Working through bitter feelings, yes, that's relevant, but forgiving is not automatically an issue.

Here's where forgiveness is always necessary – when reconciliation is desired. That doesn't mean I forgive you first. It means I'm willing to work toward a set of conditions in which forgiveness makes sense so that we can be reconciled. Justice has standards. It doesn't go around saying, "Everything's behind us. We're good. Everything is fine."

Kaka: It's hard for me to understand how a victim of a terrible offense can forgive without the other person's participation. Until I face the other person, I cannot say with all honesty that I have forgiven. I can accept that some Hutus were influenced by what would happen to them if they didn't take part in the killings. Others were particularly influenced by propaganda. But I would have a hard time understanding the kind of pressure someone has to be under to rape several women over a period of three months, to torture those individuals before they kill them, to hold Tutsi women in their houses against their will and rape them repeatedly, make them sick and impregnate them. Those things that were happening all over the country. I don't think the perpetrators were under pressure to commit most of those acts. I'm not inclined to try to forgive them. I don't have that need.

But I welcome those who have hurt me to show their remorse and to ask me to forgive them. I would like to hear more cases where offenders have come forward and admitted their crimes, faced justice, showed remorse and asked individual survivors for forgiveness. This is the key to true reconciliation between a survivor and perpetrator, but it's not an overnight process and the fruits of reconciliation would have to be determined over time.

Max: Suppose a Hutu extremist comes to my house and chases my father out the back door and overtakes him and chops him to death. A year goes by. I'm constantly eaten up by anger. I want to get my hands around that killer's throat. I want to see him dead. A Buddhist priest visits me and says, "Max, you will never heal until you forgive your father's killer." So I forgive my father's killer. Supposedly.

Another killer comes to my house. He pulls my mother out and beats her to death with the ntampangano. A year goes by and I'm internally destroyed, full of fury. I want the killer dead. A Hindu wise woman visits me and says, "Max, I know this sounds impossible, but you will always be a prisoner of your mother's killer unless you forgive him." So I forgive the killer. Supposedly.

A third killer comes to my door. This time he kills my sister. Five years go by. I am consumed with hatred for the killers, all of them. I want each of them dead as dead can be! But first I want to chop them up piece by piece. The Pope drops by and says, "Max, I heard of the horrible injuries to you and your loved ones. I know this sounds crazy, but you can forgive and find freedom from the understandable hatred that controls you. Unless you forgive all these killers, you will forever be their prisoner."

You're not going to hear the Pope talk that way, and you probably won't hear the other two talk that way, but I'm making a point about the value and the purpose of forgiveness. Forgiveness is no cheap handout. It happens when conditions are right. In situations where a wound persists, we may find that we simply aren't able to forgive. We might finally come to the place where we forgive the killers, but that doesn't mean God and everyone else does. That's an interesting thing to think about. Justice has standards.

Kaka: Around 2006 or 2007, Stella and I and four friends went to a Rwandan wedding in in the United States. The bride was Hutu-Tusti. The groom was Hutu. So Hutus and Tutsis were present. Toward the end of the reception, I was coming out of the bathroom and was met by a bigger, mid-forties man I suspected to be a Hutu who may have been active in the 1994 genocide. He could tell I was Tutsi. He got in my face and asked, "What's your name?"

I didn't answer.

He said, "Where do you live?"

I said, "Why are you asking where I live?"

"No!" he said. "You tell me where you live!"

A friend saw the rudeness and asked me, "What's going on?" He pulled me away. "Some of the perpetrators are here," my friend said. When I walked away, the Hutu said, "We will find where you live!" In Kinyarwanda, he meant *us* plural. The group I came with left immediately.

Max: Your point is, again, that forgiveness and reconciliation require the perpetrator's cooperation.

Kaka: Yes. One of my cousins was recently poisoned. He's still paralyzed. And I told you about a guy who was my brother Rangira's age. He was poisoned after trying to reconcile with his Hutu "friends." Some perpetrators are not interested in forgiveness and reconciliation.

I too believe that the fact that I would not take revenge on the killers if I had a chance – even if I wouldn't get in trouble with the law – I think this in itself is forgiving them. But it's a different type of forgiveness and should not be used to mislead people into thinking that I have forgiven those who killed my family.

Max: It's a level of forgiveness. You've done all you can do. My favorite part about you is your daily prayer asking God to help you be good to all who cross your path. It's practical and helpful. It doesn't throw an unacceptable burden on a survivor, because all of us can learn to deal with one day at a time. But, again, forgiveness doesn't have to become the issue. Tell about Michel, the attendant at Rwabuzisoni's Bar, who took Cousin Safari and you four kids in one night.

Kaka: Rwabuzisoni killed all of Michel's immediate family and then Michel's uncle's family. Michel ran away and hid for several days after he found out what his boss was doing. He didn't eat while he was hiding. His boss's wife brought him back to the bar and hid him in the house. She didn't agree with her husband's horrible acts. But Michel was afraid Rwabuzisoni would find him there, and after twenty minutes, when the rain started, Michel left. Rwabuzisoni was eventually charged with the murders and put in prison. He's out now. Do you think Michel is going to move back to the neighborhood and try to reconcile?

Max: That's not his burden to carry. He doesn't have anyone to return to.

Kaka: He would like to visit Rwabuzisoni's wife and thank her for saving his life – Michel's life – but he has no desire to see or talk to Rwabuzisoni. Michel moved near the border with Uganda, about a two-hour drive from his earlier home. His boss' wife also separated from her husband.

Max: It's very strange. Rwabuzisoni and other killers were able to move back to their homes, but the Tutsis who used to live there were either dead or unwilling to go back, just like you didn't go back to your neighborhood.

Kaka: Michel is distancing himself from his family's killer as a way to forget him so he can move on with his life. I can't imagine Michel living next-door to him or even in the same neighborhood again. This is an example of what survivors have to deal with.

What does Michel do if he doesn't have any other place to go? Is he forced to go make peace with his family's killer so he can go back and live where he lived before? His family had farm land he could benefit from, but Michel probably sold it and left town so he can stay away from his former boss and other killers like him who have served their sentences and are out of prison. He probably doesn't feel safe returning to what was home. He'd have to rebuild. I would be afraid of getting killed despite any security that may be available in town.

Max: He wouldn't go back, even if local police guaranteed his safety.

Kaka: I was standing on the road in front of Aunt Josephine's house one day after the genocide, waiting for a motorcycle to come by. It was a quicker and cheaper way of transportation around the city. I saw a motorcycle coming in the distance and flagged the driver. As he got closer, I saw that it was a boutique owner who had killed lots of Tutsis, including our family friends that lived by him. He is the same person who told my brother Rangira early in the genocide that if he ever needed a place to hide, he would keep Rangira safe. He probably would have ended up killing my brother, but Rangira ran to the RPF camp on Rebero. That man never expressed any regret to the survivors of the people he killed. When I saw him coming on the motorcycle, I took off running. No way was I going to put myself in his hands.

Max: Your former classmate Mimi saw trouble coming after her friend's little brother showed her the stash of machetes in a building behind their house. She tried to get her dad to move away before the Hutu neighbors could slice them up. When you and I met with her, she told us she ran into your brother Standard's killer – Karegeya – in prison of all places. She went there with a friend in 2005 to buy a painting for her sister's wedding present. That was something the prison offered. Prisoners could use their talents to make things and keep themselves busy with things they enjoyed doing.

Mimi said she and her friend went to the woodworking section first and saw a man dressed in pink, with really nice shoes. It was Karegeya. And as you've told me, he must have been guilty of a lot of killing to be in prison for ten years at that point. The justice system was overloaded by the extremely large number of people guilty of committing atrocities. Most prisoners served one to several years, but ten years was on the high side, and we don't know when Karegeya actually got out.

Kaka: Mimi said Karegeya wasn't sorry about anything. She said he laughed about the accusations against him, and he even seemed at peace. He said every prisoner in the facility was better off by knowing him, because they could enjoy simple benefits like lying down and taking breaks when they wanted. Karegeya seemed to want the ladies to spread a good word about him on the outside. Mimi asked how he got his super nice shoes and he said, "I have friends overseas who are always sending me things." He also wore high-end perfume.

Karegeya told Mimi the only reason he was in prison was because he used to hang out with the sons of a prominent person in the government.

Some reconciliation is happening in Rwanda. The government there encourages a smart process of bringing Rwandans together. Time will tell how successful it is. Maybe a few more generations will have to pass before the people are able to bridge the horrific treachery. We remember what one female survivor said: "It would be nice if [the abicanyi and their families] would beg us for forgiveness and tell us where the bodies are." She seemed to be in the mood for forgiving – with a little help from the guilty.

Finally, we know that one pressing question people ask is, "How can God let things like the genocide happen?" We reply by asking, When's the last time you saw people shake their fists in rage at God, the government or the universe for allowing them to tell a lie, trash somebody's reputation, cheat on a spouse, cheat an employer out of an honest day's work, withhold assistance from a needy neighbor, ruin another person's day, harass an employee, exercise a little road rage, drive intoxicated, wreck a parent's car, or ignore or scream at somebody for no good reason?

PHOTOGRAPHS

what we had, and what we hold in our hearts

We had one white cow. It looked like this one and it was a mean

beast. It was the only cow we had that would butt us with its head if we stood too close in front of it. Maybe that's why Papa kept the horns cut and cauterized. We didn't dare pat this grouchy animal. She produced good drinking milk for us, and lived a long life.

Nice Cow's brown hide looked like this one's. She was my favorite cow to be around. ⎯⎯⎯⎯→

Below, her horns were especially impressive from a side view.

All of these cow pictures are stock photos, not our actual cattle.

We also had a light brown cow. It had been with us for about a year before the genocide began. Nice Cow was dead and gone when our

light brown one came. I considered it a good replacement. Light brown was an unusual color for a cow in our neighborhood.

A cow is often given in appreciation for a big favor. One of Papa's brothers gave him a black and white cow. Cattle are a major gift, and a Rwandan groom will give one or more to the parents of his bride as a dowry during a traditional ceremony.

Back view of the smaller house. Some of us kids slept in it until Mr. Habimana and his construction crew expanded our main house. Our hired hand lived in the smaller one, which also had a storage room.

Front view of the little house. The town of Nyamirambo is in the background. Getting there from our home was about an hour's walk on a path that weaved through various kinds of plantations (fields of crops).

Another front view of the smaller house. Mr. Habimana and his crew  were remodeling it right before the massacres started. Neighbors took the new roof and the windows and doors. We paid to have them all replaced. Then we started paying a man from another town to maintain our property while living in the house. The two doors and the windows are open in this photo, although one window is hidden by the tree.

We knew which neighbors had our belongings when some of us returned after the genocide, but we didn't want anything back. We wanted our slain family members back. Our neighbors weren't ashamed to tell us who took our things, and those who took them weren't ashamed either. They never returned anything to us.

A segment of our cow pen is leaning at the left of the house. We put the cows in the pen when evening came, and we let them out in the morning.

In front of the smaller dwelling was our five-bedroom house. Mr. Habimana added two bedrooms, the family room and a balcony. Jolie was engaged to the man who, shortly after the genocide, is standing by the destroyed house. The lower part of the photo shows the top step you see in the next photo.

I was sorry to see the new construction reduce the size of our playground, where my brothers and I spent a lot of time playing soccer and I practiced juggling the ball and bouncing it against the walls of the house when I was alone. But I was happy that the extra rooms in the main house allowed us all to sleep under the same roof.

The new family room was nice because, before and after dinner, my parents gathered all of us kids into it, and Jolie always came up with different games to pass the time, especially during vacation. Not long after the meal, Papa led us in prayers and sent us to bed.

The front balcony gave our house a fancy look and served as a fun hangout sometimes when we weren't playing soccer in our shrunken playground. The excitement of our newly remodeled home lasted only several months. Then the house was violently returned to the soil it came from. Between 1992 and 1994, prior to the genocide, my parents took in six of our cousins who fled their districts because of persecution by extremists. Maybe that's why my parents upgraded the house. At one time during those two years, we were a household of close to twenty people.

1989, on the day Ingabire and Leaticau celebrated Confirmation at church. Front row, with feet on the ground: me, Dada, Stella. Middle from left: Polie, Leaticau, Rangira, Ingabire, Standard holding Rousseau, Jolie. Back row: Uncle Ephraim (Ingabire's godfather), Papa, Maman Paul, Kamuhanda (Leaticau's godfather), Safari. Damas and Jean-Marie were overseas studying. Cousin Safari is one of Kimisange's heroes who, with his good friend Butera and a couple of other friends, fought off abicanyi who came to kill hundreds of Tutsis driven from their homes. The RPF (rebel) army was only several miles away, but was not yet conducting assaults or rescue missions in the daylight.

Some Tutsis refused to open the doors for the RPF army when its soldiers tried to rescue them from churches where they were hiding. They didn't believe the rebels were actually trying to help them. The soldiers had to force their way in. Rescue operations, especially in Kigali, the capital, were very dangerous for both the RPF and the hundreds of Tutsis they were sneaking out of churches, because the rebels hadn't yet captured Kigali. A dangerous and large Hutu army was based in the heart of the city, but the RPF still managed to save thousands of urban residents hiding in churches and houses.

Above, about 1992, Papa is on the left, with Cousin Safari's little brother Yatora between Papa and Ma Paul. Stella's godmother and her husband stand with Stella in between. We were celebrating the two children's First Communion.

Baptism, First Communion, and Confirmation were always big days in our family. Relatives and friends were invited (some are seen in the background). Dowry ceremonies were a big deal too, like when Jolie's fiancé brought my family some cows and asked to marry her.

You can see the traditional wall or fence that surrounded many homes. Since it's made of vegetation, it requires more maintenance than a modern fence. These fences are high, easily up to eight feet.

Five of the people standing in the top photo were killed. It's the same story for many of these pictures. These few pictures are all we have of many loves ones, besides memories.

Teachers at one of the two primary schools where Papa taught and was principal.

My surviving siblings, their spouses and children, and I visited Mutoyi, my father's first home after he married. His first six children lived there. Extremists drove them out in the early 1970s. The big rock was a play area and a good spot to watch for Papa walking home from work. The house was several yards down from the rock.

171

Standard leaning on the doorway of his apartment. Polie bought that black shirt and the shorts for him while she was on summer vacation in Amsterdam in July 1992.

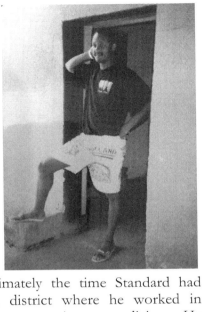

Below, at some friends' home, Standard (second to the oldest of my siblings) stands with Stella (the youngest sister) and Rousseau (the youngest of all). This was approximately the time Standard had moved back home from a Kigali district where he worked in veterinary medicine. He left that district after Hutu extremists threatened to kill him. You can see the happiness in the little ones' faces to be able to spend time with their big, big brother. Knowing him as I do, he had probably taken them out to have some fun in the city. He was a loving, older brother who helped nurture and mentor us younger brothers and sisters. He was like a father, eighteen years older than me and twenty-four years older than Rousseau.

Maman Paul holds Polie's diploma on graduation dat at Saint Andre High School. I was the only one in my family who didn't skip school to attend her graduation party at home. I went to school to receive my report card, certain that I would be called in front of the entire student body as the first in my class. It was a big school. Every grade, one through eight, had at least four different classrooms, and each classroom had about thirty students. So, there were close to a thousand students.

This was my day! I was going to be recognized for a big accomplishment that all students wanted. We all competed hard for it. I had seen some of my older brothers get in trouble for lower grades, and I knew my parents were going to pour on the praise when I got home. I was going to get a lot of praise from my parents when i got home. When I got there, everyone teased me, saying, "Ahhh, now we see why you didn't want to come to your sister's graduation. You didn't want to miss a recognition at school."

The recognition meant the world to me. So did the new soccer ball Standard awarded me. He offered me the choice of new shoes or the bright-yellow ball with black dots around it. I chose the ball. My older brothers said I should've chosen new shoes, but I was tired of playing with a ball we made out of a bunch of plastic bags we tied together with string that was not always available. Sometimes we used moist fibers from a banana plant, but the fibers soon dried and the ball would fall apart. Also, the handmade ball didn't bounce, which made it not so fun to play with.

My brothers were the first ones to ask if they could use my new ball. We all loved the way it bounced. I let them use it, and they allowed me to play with them. They picked on me less after that. I never took the ball to school. It would've been stolen in a heartbeat, or the older kids might have taken it. I had little protection, since my older brothers attended a different school at the time. So, my classmates and I went on playing with the ball made out of plastic bags, the one that didn't bounce. Anyway, if ever there happened to be a nicer, bouncing soccer ball at school, the upper grades were using it, not the lower ones.

For a long time prior to the genocide, it didn't matter whether Tutsis made good grades. They were denied admittance to public schools and universities. Some who were accepted were placed in worse schools, such as boarding schools far from home, and some of them were harassed and beaten by extremists. One boy I knew was beaten and came back home with a broken arm. He never went back to that school.

Right, Jolie adjusts Papa's jacket during Polie's high school graduation party in our front yard. Left, Polie chats with her math teacher and family friend, Theoneste Mutsindashyaka, who is trying on a necklace that Polie received as a graduation gift. Theoneste said Papa cared a lot about students and used to ask, "What's the best way I can teach my students math so they can know it?"

Right, Jolie sent Polie this studio portrait when Polie was studying in Switzerland. Jolie is posing in an outfit designed for her high school graduation party.

Jolie and Standard enjoy a meal together in Baoba, Nyamirambo.

The earliest photo we have of Ma Paul.
The same picture used to be on her ID card.

Papa signs for Jolie's court wedding, a ceremony to which twenty to thirty family members and close friends are invited. Two witnesses each from families of the bride and groom sign on the certificate. Normally, the court wedding falls between Tuesday and Friday, and the church wedding is on that same weekend or the following weekend. Some couples wait longer to tie the knot.

Polie received this picture after the genocide. Her friend Anastase Seruvumba intended to mail it to her. He lived in Switzerland and was doing his university research in Rwanda. He never made it back to Geneva. He was apparently killed the night Rwandan President Habyarimana's plane was shot down.

Papa holds a calabasse (gourd) during a cousin's dowry ceremony.
The calebasse holds the traditional Rwandan banana beer.

Below, some of my relatives stand in front of the familiar wall
that surrounded many rural homes. Styles vary slightly.

CITED SOURCES

We consulted with numerous people and publications for fact-checking this story. The following publications were cited.

Carl Wilkens, *I'm Not Leaving.* (ImNotLeavingRwanda.com, 2011).

Roméo Dallaire, *Shake Hands with the Devil: The Failure of Humanity in Rwanda* (Canada: Random House, 2003).

Ros Wynne-Jones, "Rwanda Heroes: 17 Years On", *The Guardian.* (Online magazine, 2011).

ABOUT THE AUTHORS

Kagabo Kayiranga (Kaka) Jean-Léonard moved to America in 1998 at age 17. Unable to speak or understand English, he was placed as a freshman at Brandywine Junior-Senior High School in Niles, Michigan. He managed to graduate at the end of his junior year and then began working toward his B.S. in biotechnology. He currently works as a senior analytical chemist in research. His wife Diane Umulisa Kagabo moved to America from Rwanda in 2016. Their firstborn, Zaiyn Jacob Ndindabahizi Kagabo, was born in September 2018. Kaka's favorite Rwandan dish is peanut flower stew, isombe and rice. His favorite American food is pasta – particularly, lasagna. He enjoys playing soccer, basketball and ping pong, and spending time with family and friends. He lives in the Indianapolis area.

Max T. Russell lives in the Indianapolis area too. As a specialist in human learning and memory, he helps professionals fifty years and older figure out who they are "at this point" in their work, and what they want to do next. He has written numerous articles for the nonprofit and business-intelligence communities.